RAISING KIDS IN A DIGITAL WORLD:

A Parent's Guide to Combating Cyberbullying Through Awareness and Kindness

Alexa Blake

© **Copyright 2024 - All rights reserved.**

The content contained within this book may not be reproduced, duplicated or transmitted without direct written permission from the author or the publisher.

Under no circumstances will any blame or legal responsibility be held against the publisher, or author, for any damages, reparation, or monetary loss due to the information contained within this book, either directly or indirectly.

Legal Notice:

This book is copyright protected. It is only for personal use. You cannot amend, distribute, sell, use, quote or paraphrase any part, or the content within this book, without the consent of the author or publisher.

Disclaimer Notice:

Please note the information contained within this document is for educational and entertainment purposes only. All effort has been executed to present accurate, up to date, reliable, complete information. No warranties of any kind are declared or implied. Readers acknowledge that the author is not engaged in the rendering of legal, financial, medical or professional advice. The content within this book has been derived from various sources. Please consult a licensed professional before attempting any techniques outlined in this book.

By reading this document, the reader agrees that under no circumstances is the author responsible for any losses, direct or indirect, that are incurred as a result of the use of the information contained within this document, including, but not limited to, errors, omissions, or inaccuracies.

Table of Contents

Introduction: 1
Entering the Digital Jungle 1
   What is Cyberbullying? 1
   Why Cyberbullying is a Growing Concern 2
   Purpose of This Guide 4
Part I: 7
Understanding the Scope of Cyberbullying .. 7
Chapter 1: 9
Different Forms of Cyberbullying 9
   Types of Cyberbullying 10
   Where It Happens 14
Chapter 2: 17
The Emotional Impact of Cyberbullying 17
   Short-Term Effects 17
Chapter 3: 25
Cyberbullying at Different Ages 25
   Younger Children (Ages 6-10) 25
   Tweens and Teens (Ages 11-18) 28
Part II: 33
Recognizing the Warning Signs 33
Chapter 4: 35
Spotting if Your Child is Being Cyberbullied 35
   Behavioral Changes 35

Online Behavior Shifts 39
Chapter 5: 43
Signs Your Child Might Be Cyberbullying Others
.... 43
    Changes in Behavior 43
    Online Behavior Shifts 48
Chapter 6: 51
The Role of Bystanders in Cyberbullying 51
    Bystanders vs. Upstanders 52
    Why Children Hesitate to Speak Up 53
    Encouraging Children to Speak Up 55
Part III: Preventing Cyberbullying 59
Chapter 7: 61
Teaching Digital Citizenship 61
    What is Digital Citizenship? 61
    Establishing Online Boundaries 63
    Respect and Empathy Online 66
Chapter 8: 69
Family Rules for Online Safety 69
    Creating a Family Media Agreement 69
    Monitoring Online Activity 72
    Setting Consequences for Misuse 75
Chapter 9: Building Emotional Resilience and Teaching Kindness 78
    What is Emotional Resilience? 78

Teaching Kindness: The Key to Positive Online and Offline Interactions 80

The Ripple Effect of Kindness in Digital Spaces 83

Developing Emotional Intelligence Through Kindness 87

Building Kindness into Daily Habits 90

Helping Children Cope: Fostering a Sense of Self-Worth 92

Part IV: 94

Responding to Cyberbullying 94

Chapter 10: 96

What to Do if Your Child is Cyberbullied 96

Talking to Your Child: Approaching the Conversation 97

Documenting and Reporting Cyberbullying .. 99

Helping Your Child Recover: Rebuilding Self-Esteem and Confidence 101

Chapter 11: 106

Addressing Cyberbullying if Your Child is the Bully 106

Confronting the Behavior: How to Approach the Situation 106

Teaching Empathy and Responsibility 109

Cultivating Empathy and Kindness at Home 112

Chapter 12: 116

How to Create a Safe and Open Online Environment at Home 116

Creating a Judgment-Free Zone 116
Building Trust with Your Child 118
Regular Family Check-ins 120
Empowering Your Child to Make Safe Choices
.... 121

Chapter 13: 124
Cyberbullying in the Era of Emerging AI .. 124
AI-Enhanced Cyberbullying Tactics 124
Impact of AI on Privacy and Cybersecurity . 126
AI and Parental Controls 127
Limitations of AI in Cyberbullying Detection:
.... 128
Practical Tips for Parents 130

Conclusion: 132
Navigating the Future of Cyberbullying 132
The Importance of Staying Informed 132
Final Thoughts: Helping Your Child Navigate the Digital World 135
Resources for Parents and Children 137

Appendix: 139
Sample Family Media Agreement 139
Glossary: 143
References 147

Introduction:
Entering the Digital Jungle

In today's rapidly evolving world, children are navigating a landscape very different from the one many of us grew up in. While the internet offers opportunities for learning, connection, and creativity, it also harbors dangers that can be challenging to manage, especially for young minds. Among these dangers, one of the most pervasive and harmful is cyberbullying—a modern form of bullying that thrives in the digital spaces children frequent, often leaving deep emotional scars (Kowalski et al., 2014).

What is Cyberbullying?

At its core, cyberbullying refers to the use of digital technology—such as smartphones, social media platforms, messaging apps, and online games—to intimidate, harass, or humiliate another person (Hinduja & Patchin, 2015). Unlike traditional bullying, which is typically confined to school or social environments, cyberbullying knows no boundaries. It can happen anywhere, anytime, and often goes unnoticed by parents and teachers because it occurs in the virtual world. The anonymity that the internet sometimes offers emboldens bullies, making their actions even more harmful.

Cyberbullying can take many forms—spreading rumors, sending threatening messages, sharing embarrassing photos or videos without consent, or excluding someone from an online group (Smith et al., 2008). One of the most alarming aspects of cyberbullying is its potential to be relentless, as victims can be targeted around the clock, often feeling like there is no escape. Furthermore, since the abuse happens online, it can reach a much wider audience, amplifying the victim's humiliation and emotional distress.

Why Cyberbullying is a Growing Concern

Cyberbullying has become a growing concern for parents, educators, and mental health professionals alike. The rise of social media, the prevalence of smartphones, and the increasing popularity of online gaming have all contributed to this troubling trend. As children spend more time online, they become more exposed to the risks associated with unregulated digital spaces (Livingstone et al., 2011).

One reason cyberbullying is so prevalent is the increased access to technology. Children as young as six or seven often own smartphones or tablets, giving them constant access to the internet and social platforms. While these devices offer convenience and entertainment, they also open the door to potential harm. Social media platforms like Instagram, TikTok, and Snapchat allow for instant communication, where conflicts that once took place face-to-face now unfold in the digital world, often with more significant consequences.

Moreover, the anonymous nature of online interactions allows bullies to hide behind fake profiles or usernames, making it easier to engage in harmful behavior without fear of immediate repercussions (Kowalski et al., 2014). Unlike traditional bullying, which typically happens in schoolyards or classrooms where adults can intervene, cyberbullying often takes place out of sight, making it harder to detect and address.

The long-term effects of cyberbullying can be devastating. Victims may experience anxiety, depression, and low self-esteem, sometimes leading to self-harm or even suicide (Hinduja & Patchin, 2015). The emotional impact is often compounded by the fact that many children suffer in silence, either out of fear of retaliation or because they believe nothing can be done to stop it.

Purpose of This Guide

The aim of this guide is to empower parents to take an active role in combating cyberbullying, equipping them with the knowledge and tools needed to support their children in today's digital world. This book is not just about identifying the signs of cyberbullying; it's about preventing it before it happens, responding effectively when it does, and helping children develop the resilience needed to thrive in an increasingly connected world.

Throughout the chapters, we will explore how parents can create a safer online environment for their children, from teaching them responsible online behavior to setting appropriate boundaries around technology use. You'll learn how to recognize the warning signs that your child may be a victim of cyberbullying—or that they may be engaging in bullying behavior themselves. We'll also look at the crucial role of empathy and kindness in preventing bullying, both online and offline, and how these qualities can be nurtured in children to foster positive digital interactions.

Additionally, this guide offers practical advice on how to recover from the emotional wounds of cyberbullying, emphasizing the importance of building emotional resilience and a strong sense of self-worth in your child. As a parent, your role is crucial in guiding your children through the challenges of the digital age, ensuring they feel supported, empowered, and capable of navigating the opportunities and dangers of the online world.

By the end of this book, you will have a deeper understanding of the complex nature of cyberbullying, the tools to prevent and address it, and the strategies to help your child emerge stronger and more resilient. The digital jungle may be vast and untamed, but with the right knowledge and approach, we can guide our children safely through it.

Part I:

Understanding the Scope of Cyberbullying

Chapter 1:

Different Forms of Cyberbullying

In today's digital world, cyberbullying manifests in various harmful ways, each of which can significantly impact its victims emotionally and psychologically. While it shares many similarities with traditional bullying, the anonymous, constant, and far-reaching nature of online interactions allows cyberbullying to extend beyond the physical realm, creating unique challenges for those involved. The ability to harass, exclude, or impersonate others without face-to-face confrontation makes cyberbullying particularly insidious. Understanding the different forms of cyberbullying is crucial for parents and educators to recognize warning signs and intervene before lasting damage occurs. This chapter will explore the types of cyberbullying that your child may encounter online.

Types of Cyberbullying

1. Harassment

Harassment is one of the most common and damaging forms of cyberbullying. It involves sending hurtful, threatening, or abusive messages repeatedly through online platforms. These messages might target a victim's appearance, beliefs, or personal life and can quickly escalate into a flood of hateful content. Since the internet allows for instant communication, harassment can feel overwhelming as victims may receive multiple messages in a short amount of time, leaving them feeling trapped and powerless (Hinduja & Patchin, 2015).

Harassment can happen publicly, such as in social media comment sections, or privately through direct messages and emails. This form of cyberbullying is often relentless, with perpetrators aiming to break down the victim's emotional defenses over time. Unfortunately, the ease with which bullies can create new accounts means that blocking one profile doesn't always stop the harassment (Willard, 2007).

2. Exclusion

Exclusion occurs when a child is deliberately left out of online groups or activities. In the digital age, social interactions among children and teens often occur through group chats, social media, and online gaming communities. Being excluded from these spaces can lead to feelings of isolation and rejection, especially when it's done in a public way, such as leaving someone out of a group chat or unfollowing them en masse on social media (Kowalski et al., 2014).

Exclusion can sometimes be subtle, making it hard for parents to spot. For example, children might not be invited to online games or may be purposefully ignored in group conversations. This form of bullying preys on a child's need for social acceptance, creating emotional distress that can have lasting consequences on their self-esteem (Tokunaga, 2010).

3. Impersonation

Impersonation occurs when someone takes control of another person's online identity to harm them. This form of cyberbullying can be especially distressing as it involves a loss of control over one's digital self. The bully might create fake profiles, post harmful or misleading content under the victim's name, or send inappropriate messages to others pretending to be the victim.

Impersonation is dangerous because it damages the victim's reputation and can have real-world consequences. For instance, offensive messages sent under the victim's name could lead to social or academic fallout. Since the internet retains information indefinitely, these false representations can resurface even after the bullying stops (Hinduja & Patchin, 2015).

4. Outing

Outing involves sharing someone's private, sensitive, or embarrassing information, photos, or messages without their consent. This type of cyberbullying often aims to publicly humiliate the victim by exposing details that were intended to remain private. Whether sharing a personal conversation or posting a humiliating photo, outing violates trust and can be deeply damaging.

The emotional consequences of outing can include feelings of betrayal, shame, and vulnerability. In some cases, the public exposure of private information can even escalate to legal issues or physical harm (Cassidy et al., 2013).

5. Cyberstalking

Cyberstalking is an extreme form of harassment where the bully tracks and intimidates the victim through persistent and often threatening messages, comments, or posts. It may involve obsessively following someone's activities across different social media platforms or messaging them repeatedly despite being asked to stop (Willard, 2007).

This type of cyberbullying creates a sense of fear and helplessness, as victims often feel they are constantly being watched and harassed. The psychological effects of cyberstalking can be profound, making the victim feel unsafe both online and offline.

6. Trolling

Trolling refers to the deliberate posting of inflammatory, irrelevant, or off-topic comments with the intent of provoking others and causing conflict. Trolls often target vulnerable individuals, disrupting conversations and escalating tension. While trolling may seem less severe than other forms of bullying, it can cause significant emotional harm, especially when sensitive topics are exploited to distress others (Hinduja & Patchin, 2015).

Where It Happens

1. Social Media Platforms

Platforms like Instagram, TikTok, Snapchat, and Facebook are the most common arenas for cyberbullying. These social networks allow users to post comments, share media, and interact in ways that can quickly turn toxic. Public profiles can make it easier for bullies to spread harmful content, and direct messaging features enable private harassment.

2. Messaging Apps

Apps such as WhatsApp, iMessage, and Discord allow for private communication, where cyberbullying often goes unnoticed by adults. Group chats can be breeding grounds for exclusion, name-calling, and rumor-spreading, especially when multiple children gang up on a single victim (Cassidy et al., 2013).

3. Online Gaming Communities

Gaming platforms like Roblox, Fortnite, and Minecraft are popular with children and teens but can also be environments where cyberbullying thrives. Verbal harassment over headsets, exclusion from group play, and sabotaging another player's success are common forms of bullying in these spaces (Tokunaga, 2010). Competitive environments can quickly escalate into aggressive behavior, making them ripe for bullying.

Understanding the different forms of cyberbullying and the spaces where they occur is the first step in helping parents and guardians create safer digital environments for their children. Recognizing these signs and addressing them early can prevent long-term emotional harm and foster healthier online interactions for young users.

Chapter 2:

The Emotional Impact of Cyberbullying

The emotional toll of cyberbullying can be profound, as the constant exposure to negativity and harassment leaves deep psychological scars. Unlike traditional bullying, which may occur in specific settings, cyberbullying often follows the victim everywhere through their devices. This pervasive nature makes it difficult for victims to find a safe space or escape. Understanding both the short-term and long-term emotional consequences is crucial for recognizing the seriousness of cyberbullying and taking appropriate action to protect affected children (Hinduja & Patchin, 2015).

Short-Term Effects

1. Anxiety

One of the most immediate effects of cyberbullying is anxiety. Victims often feel a sense of dread each time they receive a notification or message, fearing what hurtful words or content might await them. Since cyberbullying can happen at any time—during school, at home, or even while relaxing—children may become hyper-vigilant, constantly worrying about being attacked online (Campbell et al., 2018). This persistent state of anxiety can interfere with their concentration, sleep, and daily functioning.

Anxiety often manifests physically as well, with children experiencing symptoms such as headaches, stomachaches, and restlessness. They may become jittery or avoid activities that involve online interactions, such as participating in social media or online games, which can further isolate them from their peers.

2. Stress

In the short term, cyberbullying can cause high levels of stress. Victims often feel overwhelmed by the negative attention they receive, especially when the bullying comes from multiple sources or spreads across various platforms. The stress of managing the situation, coupled with the fear of what might come next, can take a serious toll on a child's mental well-being (Hamm et al., 2015).

Cyberbullying also triggers stress responses in the body, leading to elevated cortisol levels. This can make victims more irritable, fatigued, and less able to handle everyday challenges. They may also begin to feel a loss of control, as the situation might escalate quickly with one viral post or comment, making it feel impossible to contain the damage (Wright & Wachs, 2019).

3. Sadness and Hopelessness

One of the most pervasive immediate effects of cyberbullying is a deep sense of sadness. Victims may feel crushed by the constant negativity aimed at them, leading to feelings of hopelessness about their situation (Kowalski et al., 2014). Sadness arises not just from the hurtful words themselves but also from a loss of trust in others, especially if the bullying involves people they consider friends.

The feelings of hopelessness are exacerbated by the permanence of digital interactions. Unlike verbal insults that may fade with time, written words, screenshots, and posts can linger online, making the victim feel like the bullying will never fully go away. This can lead to feelings of powerlessness, as victims begin to doubt whether anyone can truly help them or make the bullying stop.

Long-Term Consequences

1. Depression

Over time, the emotional pain caused by cyberbullying can deepen into more serious mental health issues, such as depression. Depression is a common long-term consequence for victims who have been relentlessly targeted online. The constant exposure to hurtful comments, exclusion, or malicious rumors can erode their sense of self-worth, leading to persistent feelings of sadness, apathy, and hopelessness (Hinduja & Patchin, 2015).

Depression may also manifest physically, with victims showing a lack of energy, appetite changes, and sleep disturbances. In some cases, depression can lead to more severe outcomes, such as self-harm or suicidal thoughts, making it critical to address cyberbullying early to prevent it from escalating to this point.

2. Low Self-Esteem

Another significant long-term consequence of cyberbullying is the erosion of self-esteem. Children who are repeatedly targeted online may begin to internalize the negative messages they receive, believing that they are worthless, unattractive, or undeserving of love and respect

(Campbell et al., 2018). This gradual breakdown of their self-image can have lasting effects on their confidence and ability to navigate social situations.

Low self-esteem can impact a child's academic performance, relationships, and willingness to engage with the world around them. Victims may struggle with feelings of inadequacy or develop a belief that they are to blame for the bullying. This low self-esteem can sometimes carry over into adulthood, affecting their career choices, romantic relationships, and overall life satisfaction.

3. Social Isolation

One of the more damaging long-term effects of cyberbullying is social isolation. Victims often withdraw from social interactions as a way to protect themselves from further harm. They may avoid participating in group activities, stop using social media, or distance themselves from friends out of fear of being bullied again (Hamm et al., 2015). This self-imposed isolation, while a coping mechanism, can exacerbate feelings of loneliness and alienation.

Social isolation can also lead to difficulties in forming and maintaining healthy relationships. Victims may struggle to trust others, fearing that new friendships or relationships will only lead to more pain. Over time, this isolation can contribute to mental health issues such as depression and anxiety, creating a vicious cycle that becomes harder to break as the victim retreats further from social engagement (Wright & Wachs, 2019).

4. Difficulty Trusting Others

Cyberbullying often involves a betrayal of trust, especially when the bully is someone the victim once considered a friend. This breach of trust can have long-lasting repercussions, making it difficult for the victim to open up to others in the future (Kowalski et al., 2014). They may become overly guarded, skeptical, or cynical about people's intentions, fearing that anyone could turn against them at any time.

Trust issues can spill over into all areas of the victim's life, from friendships and family relationships to romantic partnerships and professional collaborations. The inability to trust others can lead to a sense of emotional isolation, as victims may keep their guard up to avoid being hurt again.

5. Post-Traumatic Stress Disorder (PTSD)

In extreme cases, the trauma caused by cyberbullying can lead to the development of Post-Traumatic Stress

Disorder (PTSD). Victims who experience severe or prolonged cyberbullying may relive the distressing events through flashbacks or nightmares, particularly if the bullying involved public humiliation or threats of physical harm. They may also experience heightened anxiety, hypervigilance, and avoidance behaviors, such as steering clear of certain online platforms or social settings that remind them of the bullying (Campbell et al., 2018).

PTSD from cyberbullying can significantly impair a child's ability to function in their daily life. They may have trouble concentrating at school, interacting with peers, or engaging in activities they once enjoyed. Early intervention and support are essential in mitigating these long-term effects and helping victims regain their sense of safety and control (Wright et al., 2019).

The emotional impact of cyberbullying is far-reaching, with both immediate and lasting consequences that can severely affect a child's well-being. From the onset of anxiety and sadness to the development of long-term issues like depression and social isolation, the damage inflicted by cyberbullying extends beyond the digital realm into the victim's emotional and psychological health. Recognizing these effects early and providing appropriate support can make a crucial difference in helping children navigate and recover from the harm caused by cyberbullying.

Chapter 3:

Cyberbullying at Different Ages

Cyberbullying affects children differently at various stages of development, with younger children often experiencing subtle forms of online cruelty and older children facing more direct, aggressive interactions. Understanding how cyberbullying manifests at different ages can help parents and educators recognize early signs, intervene effectively, and provide appropriate support tailored to a child's developmental needs.

Younger Children (Ages 6-10)

At this stage, many children are just beginning to explore the digital world, often under parental supervision. While younger children may not be as active on social media platforms, they can still experience cyberbullying in other online spaces, such as gaming communities or messaging apps used for group activities (Livingstone & Smith, 2014).

1. **Exclusion from Games**

One common form of cyberbullying among younger children is exclusion from online games or activities. Children in this age group may be left out of multiplayer games or denied access to in-game chat groups, often without explanation. The digital nature of these games means that exclusion can happen quickly, and once the child is excluded, they may feel powerless to rejoin the group (Hinduja & Patchin, 2015).

For a young child, being left out can feel deeply personal and hurtful. It taps into their desire for social acceptance and belonging. This exclusion can lead to feelings of rejection, loneliness, and confusion, as they may not fully understand why they were singled out (Willard, 2007). Parents should monitor their child's online gaming interactions, watching for signs of distress, such as reluctance to play or sudden shifts in mood after playing with peers online.

2. **Teasing and Name-Calling**

Teasing is another way cyberbullying shows up in younger children's lives. This might involve sending hurtful messages through messaging apps or making fun of someone during in-game chat sessions. Young children might call each other names, make fun of each other's appearance, or criticize someone's gaming skills, often without realizing the lasting emotional damage they are causing (Kowalski et al., 2014).

While teasing might seem like harmless child's play to some, it can quickly escalate into more serious forms of bullying. Name-calling and mocking can deeply affect a young child's self-esteem, especially when it comes from friends or peers they admire. The anonymity or distance provided by digital platforms may make children feel more emboldened to say things they wouldn't dare to say in person (Livingstone & Smith, 2014).

3. Fear and Confusion

Cyberbullying in younger children often leaves them feeling confused and scared. They may not have the emotional vocabulary to express how they feel or fully understand why they are being targeted. This confusion can cause them to withdraw from activities they once enjoyed or become anxious when interacting with peers online. Children may also struggle to explain the situation to their parents, not knowing how to describe what's happening (Willard, 2007).

Parents should create an open line of communication with their children, encouraging them to talk about their online experiences. It's important to listen carefully and without judgment to help younger children navigate these early encounters with cyberbullying and teach them how to handle exclusion or teasing in a healthy way (Hinduja & Patchin, 2015).

Tweens and Teens (Ages 11-18)

As children enter their tween and teenage years, cyberbullying tends to become more prevalent and aggressive, often linked to peer pressure, social media interactions, and the desire to fit in. Tweens and teens are more likely to be deeply embedded in online communities, using social media, messaging apps, and video-sharing platforms to maintain friendships, gain popularity, or seek validation (Kowalski et al., 2014).

1. Social Media and Peer Pressure

Social media has become a significant arena for cyberbullying among tweens and teens. Platforms like Instagram, TikTok, Snapchat, and others allow users to post, comment, and interact with one another in ways that can easily turn malicious. For instance, a teen might post a photo and receive hurtful comments about their appearance, or they could be the target of a cruel "meme" or edited photo shared to humiliate them (Willard, 2007).

Peer pressure amplifies the risks of cyberbullying in this age group. The desire to gain social approval can push tweens and teens to participate in bullying behavior themselves, even if they don't feel comfortable with it. They might join in on a group chat making fun of someone or "like" hurtful comments to avoid being singled out themselves. The fear of losing social standing or being isolated can make cyberbullying seem like a way to fit in or protect their reputation (Livingstone & Smith, 2014).

2. Group Chats and Private Messages

Private group chats or messaging apps are often where the most harmful forms of cyberbullying occur. In these private spaces, teens may engage in gossip, spread rumors, or share embarrassing information about someone without fear of public scrutiny. The closed nature of these chats makes it difficult for outsiders, including parents, to detect the bullying, allowing it to go unchecked for long periods of time (Hinduja & Patchin, 2015).

3. Impersonation and Spreading Rumors

As tweens and teens become more digitally savvy, impersonation and rumor-spreading become common tactics in cyberbullying. A bully might create a fake social media account posing as the victim, posting harmful content, or sending rude messages in their name. This form of impersonation can damage a teen's reputation and create significant emotional distress, especially if the fake account spreads rapidly through their social circles (Kowalski et al., 2014).

4. Sexting and Threats of Exposure

One of the most devastating forms of cyberbullying that emerges in the teen years is related to sexting and the non-consensual sharing of intimate images. Teens may be pressured to send explicit photos to someone they trust, only to have those photos used against them later. This form of cyberbullying can involve threats of exposure— where the bully threatens to share the images with others if the victim doesn't comply with certain demands—or outright sharing the images with peers to humiliate the victim (Hinduja & Patchin, 2015).

The psychological damage from this kind of bullying is severe, often leading to deep shame, fear, and social withdrawal. Victims of such harassment may feel their entire world is collapsing as their private lives becomes the subject of public ridicule. The long-term consequences can include depression, PTSD, and significant damage to self-esteem (Willard, 2007).

Understanding how cyberbullying manifests at different ages helps parents and educators tailor their approach to preventing, identifying, and addressing bullying. Younger children may struggle with exclusion and teasing, while tweens and teens face more complex and aggressive forms of bullying, often amplified by social media and peer pressure. By recognizing the signs at each developmental stage, adults can provide the appropriate support and guidance needed to help children navigate the digital world safely.

Part II:

Recognizing the Warning Signs

Chapter 4:
Spotting if Your Child is Being Cyberbullied

One of the most challenging aspects of cyberbullying is that it often takes place in hidden, virtual spaces, making it difficult for parents to detect. Unlike traditional bullying, where physical signs such as bruises or face-to-face confrontations may be visible, cyberbullying leaves emotional and psychological scars that can manifest in more subtle ways. Recognizing these early warning signs is critical in helping parents intervene before the effects of cyberbullying escalate. This chapter will explore the behavioral and online shifts that may indicate your child is experiencing cyberbullying.

Behavioral Changes

When a child is being cyberbullied, their behavior often changes in noticeable ways. These changes are usually the result of emotional distress, as the child grapples with the hurtful or threatening messages they receive online. Parents should stay vigilant, paying close attention to shifts in their child's behavior patterns. Here are some common indicators that your child may be facing cyberbullying:

1. Withdrawal from Family and Friends

A child who is being cyberbullied may begin to withdraw from family activities or social interactions with friends. They might become increasingly isolated, preferring to spend time alone in their room or avoiding family meals and conversations. This withdrawal is often driven by feelings of shame, embarrassment, or fear of being judged (Kowalski et al., 2014). They may also feel powerless to explain their situation, fearing that others won't understand or might blame them for what's happening.

If your child was previously engaged and social but now avoids interacting with family members, it could be a sign that they are dealing with cyberbullying. In some cases, the child may withdraw from their peer group entirely, avoiding their friends or social gatherings that they once enjoyed.

2. Anxiety About Going to School

Since many cyberbullying incidents occur between classmates or social groups, the emotional toll can extend beyond the digital world into the physical world, such as at school. A child who is being bullied online may start to feel anxious or fearful about attending school, particularly if they know they'll encounter their bullies there (Smith et al., 2008). They may express reluctance to go to school or even feign illness to avoid facing their peers.

This anxiety often stems from a fear of confrontation or further humiliation. Even if the bullying happens exclusively online, the anticipation of seeing the bully in person can create significant stress.

3. Mood Swings and Emotional Outbursts

Children dealing with cyberbullying often experience heightened emotional sensitivity. They may have frequent mood swings, moving from sadness to anger in short periods. The stress of constant online harassment can cause children to become more irritable or defensive, leading to uncharacteristic outbursts or emotional breakdowns (Wright & Wachs, 2019). These outbursts may be triggered by seemingly small events or interactions, masking the deeper emotional turmoil they are experiencing from the cyberbullying.

Pay attention if your child seems unusually quick to anger or becomes overwhelmed by situations that normally wouldn't bother them. These mood swings could be a sign that they are bottling up emotions related to online bullying.

4. Changes in Sleep Patterns

The stress caused by cyberbullying can disrupt a child's sleep. They may have trouble falling asleep, staying asleep, or experiencing nightmares. Some children may become afraid to sleep, worrying about what will happen online while they are not actively monitoring their social media or messages (Beran & Li, 2005). Conversely, some children may sleep excessively as a way to escape the distressing reality of their online interactions.

If your child begins showing signs of insomnia, frequent waking during the night, or seems unusually tired during the day, it could be related to the stress and anxiety caused by cyberbullying.

5. Decline in Academic Performance

Cyberbullying can take a significant toll on a child's ability to focus and perform well in school. The emotional weight of being targeted online often leads to difficulties concentrating in class, completing homework, or studying for exams (Huang & Chou, 2010). If your child's grades begin to drop or if teachers report that they seem distracted, unfocused, or uninterested in schoolwork, it may be a sign that they are struggling with an issue beyond the classroom.

Parents should note if a previously diligent or academically engaged child suddenly becomes apathetic about schoolwork or starts failing subjects they once excelled in.

Online Behavior Shifts

In addition to behavioral changes, shifts in your child's online activity can also signal that they are experiencing cyberbullying. Because cyberbullying takes place in the digital realm, paying attention to how your child interacts with their devices and online platforms can provide critical clues.

1. **Avoiding Social Media and Devices:** Children who are being cyberbullied often try to avoid the source of their distress by distancing themselves from social media and devices. If your child suddenly becomes reluctant to use their phone, avoids social media platforms they used to enjoy, or expresses a desire to delete their profiles altogether, this could be a red flag (Kowalski et al., 2014). They may try to

escape the hurtful messages or harassment they receive online, but fear of further bullying or embarrassment may keep them from sharing the real reason for their avoidance.

2. **Being Secretive About Online Activity:** Another common sign of cyberbullying is secrecy around online activity. Children who are being targeted may become more guarded about what they are doing online. They might hide their screens when you walk into the room, quickly close tabs or apps, or avoid answering questions about their online interactions (Wright & Wachs, 2019). This secretive behavior is often rooted in fear—fear that their parents will find out about the bullying or that the bullying will escalate if they report it.

3. **Deleting Profiles or Posts:** If your child begins deleting social media posts, comments, or even entire accounts without explanation, this could be a reaction to cyberbullying. Victims of bullying may feel pressure to remove any content that their bullies are using to harass them, or they may feel overwhelmed by the negative responses to their posts (Huang & Chou, 2010). This could include deleting photos, changing

profile pictures frequently, or wiping their online presence entirely in an attempt to protect themselves.

4. **Sudden Increase in Time Spent Online:** On the flip side, some children may spend more time online in response to cyberbullying, constantly checking messages or social media accounts for updates from their bullies. They may feel the need to monitor the situation closely, afraid of what the bully will post or say next (Beran & Li, 2005). This can lead to obsessive checking of notifications, late-night screen time, and increased anxiety around their online interactions.

Recognizing these warning signs can help parents intervene before cyberbullying causes deeper emotional and psychological harm. By staying attuned to changes in your child's behavior and online activity, you can open a dialogue and offer the support they need to navigate the complexities of the digital world.

Chapter 5:

Signs Your Child Might Be Cyberbullying Others

While much of the focus in discussions about cyberbullying is on how to identify and help victims, it is equally important to recognize the signs that your child might be engaging in bullying behavior online. The digital environment can empower children to act in ways they may not consider in face-to-face interactions, given the perceived anonymity and distance provided by the internet. If left unchecked, cyberbullying can have long-term consequences not only for the victim but also for the perpetrator (Kowalski et al., 2014).

This chapter will explore the behavioral and online shifts that may indicate your child is involved in cyberbullying others, helping parents recognize the warning signs and intervene before further harm is done.

Changes in Behavior

Children who engage in cyberbullying often exhibit shifts in their behavior that can be subtle at first but become more noticeable over time. It's essential to understand that children who bully others may not always fit the stereotype of an "aggressive" or "bad" kid. They may come from loving homes, have good grades, and appear well-adjusted in many ways. However, changes in their demeanor, social interactions, and how they approach technology can offer clues (Smith et al., 2008).

1. Becoming More Secretive About Online Activity

Just as children who are being cyberbullied may hide their online activities, children who engage in bullying may also become secretive. They might quickly close browser tabs or apps when a parent walks into the room, become defensive when asked about their online behavior, or refuse to talk about what they are doing on social media.

This secrecy can be a sign that your child is aware that their behavior is wrong, or they may be trying to avoid getting caught (Wright, 2019). For example, if they create fake accounts, send hurtful messages, or participate in group bullying, they may fear the consequences of their actions if discovered.

2. New Peer Groups and Social Dynamics

Pay attention to shifts in your child's friendships and social circles. If your child starts hanging out with a new group of friends, particularly those who seem to encourage negative behavior or gossip, it could be a sign that they are falling into a peer dynamic that promotes bullying. Peer pressure is a significant factor in bullying, especially during adolescence, where social status and group identity become central (Pellegrini & Bartini, 2000).

A child may feel compelled to participate in cyberbullying to fit in with their new friends or to avoid becoming a target themselves. They may also begin to speak about others in a more judgmental or dismissive way, reflecting the attitudes of their peer group. Comments that dehumanize or belittle others, particularly online, may indicate they are engaging in bullying behavior.

3. Displaying Aggressive or Defiant Behavior

Children who cyberbully others often exhibit increased aggression in both their online and offline interactions. This aggression might not always be physical; it can manifest as verbal outbursts, an increased tendency to argue with family members, or a general defiance towards authority. In some cases, this behavior reflects the way they communicate online, where anonymity or distance gives them the confidence to act out in ways they wouldn't in person (Archer & Coyne, 2005). This aggression can spill over into their digital interactions, where they may use harsh language, threats, or cruel jokes to belittle others.

If your child is frequently involved in online conflicts or seems to derive satisfaction from provoking others, it's important to investigate whether this behavior extends to cyberbullying.

4. Lack of Empathy Toward Others

One of the hallmarks of a child who is engaging in cyberbullying is a noticeable lack of empathy. They may dismiss the feelings of others, make jokes about someone's pain or humiliation, or fail to recognize the impact of their words and actions (Gini & Pozzoli, 2007). This emotional distance allows them to engage in bullying behavior without fully grasping the harm they are causing.

If your child seems indifferent to the emotions of others or shows no remorse after hurting someone, it's crucial to address this lack of empathy. In some cases, children who bully online may not realize the severity of their actions, especially if they believe what they are doing is "just a joke." Helping them understand the consequences of their behavior can be an essential step in curbing their bullying tendencies.

5. Sudden Boost in Social Status or Popularity

Some children engage in cyberbullying to gain popularity or assert dominance within their peer group. If your child suddenly experiences a rise in social status or becomes more popular seemingly overnight, it's worth examining the reasons behind it. They may be using bullying as a tool to increase their influence or solidify their standing among their peers (Seçilmiş & Çakır, 2017).

Popularity gained through bullying is often short-lived and harmful to both the bully and their victims. It creates an unhealthy dynamic where power and control are based on fear and exclusion. If your child's new popularity comes at the expense of others, or if they seem to enjoy making fun of classmates, it's essential to explore whether this behavior is tied to cyberbullying.

Online Behavior Shifts

Alongside changes in their offline behavior, children who are engaging in cyberbullying often display distinct shifts in how they use technology. Since cyberbullying is a digital phenomenon, paying close attention to your child's online habits can help you spot potential warning signs.

1. Frequent Use of Anonymous or Secondary Accounts

One of the common tactics used by cyberbullies is creating anonymous or secondary accounts to target their victims without revealing their identity. If your child has multiple social media profiles or frequently uses anonymous messaging apps, this could be a sign that they are engaging in cyberbullying. These accounts allow them to send hurtful messages, post embarrassing content, or impersonate others without being traced (Beran & Li, 2005).

If you notice that your child is using apps or platforms that prioritize anonymity, or if they switch between accounts frequently, it's worth investigating why they feel the need to hide their identity.

2. Spending More Time Online, Especially at Odd Hours

A child who is cyberbullying others may spend excessive time online, particularly late at night or during times when they know they won't be monitored. This behavior allows them to target their victims without the interference of parents or teachers. They may also become more protective of their devices, insisting on using them in private spaces or becoming agitated if asked to share their passwords or online activity.

If your child is increasingly secretive about their screen time or seems glued to their device in a way that disrupts their usual routines, it could indicate that they are engaging in harmful online behavior.

3. Laughing or Smiling at Their Devices

If your child is frequently laughing or smiling at their phone or computer while engaged in online conversations, it may not always be innocent. While it's normal for children to enjoy chatting with friends or sharing funny content, excessive laughter, particularly in private or when interacting with others online, could signal that they are mocking or teasing someone inappropriately.

Be cautious of interactions where your child seems to find joy in the misfortune or embarrassment of others. This kind of behavior is often tied to cyberbullying, where the goal is to provoke or humiliate the target for amusement.

4. Involvement in Online Conflicts or Drama

If your child is frequently involved in online drama—whether through social media posts, group chats, or gaming platforms—it may indicate that they are participating in bullying. Constant online conflicts, where your child is either the instigator or heavily involved, could be a red flag. Watch for signs of escalating arguments, heated exchanges, or passive-aggressive posts that target others. Recognizing these signs can be difficult for any parent, but early intervention is crucial to preventing further harm.

Chapter 6:
The Role of Bystanders in Cyberbullying

Cyberbullying doesn't just involve the bully and the victim; it often includes bystanders—those who witness the bullying but choose to do nothing. In the digital world, bystanders can play a significant role in either escalating or mitigating the harm caused by cyberbullying. Whether they stay silent, passively observe, or actively participate, their reactions influence the outcome of a bullying situation. In contrast, upstanders are individuals who step in to defend the victim, report the incident, or otherwise intervene positively. Helping children transition from passive bystanders to active upstanders is crucial in preventing the spread of cyberbullying and reducing its harmful effects (Rivers & Noret, 2010).

In this chapter, we will define the role of bystanders and upstanders, explore why some children hesitate to speak up and offer strategies to encourage children to take action and become upstanders in the face of cyberbullying.

Bystanders vs. Upstanders

Bystanders are people who witness or become aware of bullying but do not intervene. In the context of cyberbullying, bystanders can take several forms. They might:

- Ignore the bullying and scroll past it without engaging.
- Observe passively, possibly feeling bad for the victim but choosing not to act.
- Like, share, or comment on a harmful post, even if they do not directly participate in bullying.
- Talk about the incident privately, discussing it with friends or peers but doing nothing to stop it.

In many cases, bystanders may not intend to harm anyone, but their lack of action can still contribute to the bullying by making the victim feel unsupported and powerless (Kowalski et al., 2014). This silence can also embolden the bully, who might interpret the inaction as approval or acceptance of their behavior.

On the other hand, upstanders take action when they see bullying occur. They actively intervene by:

- Standing up for the victim by leaving supportive comments or defending them in group chats.

- Reporting the bullying to a trusted adult, teacher, or the platform where it's happening.
- Encouraging the bully to stop or making it clear that such behavior is not acceptable.
- Helping the victim regain their confidence and connecting them with the support they need (O'Connell et al., 2013).

Upstanders play a vital role in breaking the cycle of cyberbullying. When even one person steps in to stop the bullying or support the victim, it can have a powerful impact on the situation. Not only does it signal to the bully that their actions won't be tolerated, but it also provides the victim with a sense of solidarity, helping them feel less isolated (Wright, 2014).

Why Children Hesitate to Speak Up

While many children know that cyberbullying is wrong, they may hesitate to speak up for several reasons. Understanding these barriers is key to helping parents encourage their children to become upstanders.

1. **Fear of Retaliation:** One of the most common reasons children don't intervene in bullying situations is fear of becoming the next target (Baldry & Farrington, 2000). They may worry that if they speak

up, the bully will turn on them, especially in the digital world where it's easy to spread rumors or harass multiple people at once.

2. **Peer Pressure**: Children, particularly tweens and teens, are heavily influenced by their social circles. If their friends are participating in or condoning cyberbullying, they may feel pressure to go along with it, even if they know it's wrong. The fear of being ostracized or losing their place within a social group can keep many children from stepping in as upstanders (Pouwels et al., 2018).

3. **Lack of Confidence:** Many children don't feel equipped to handle the complexities of cyberbullying. They may worry that they'll make things worse by getting involved or may not know how to respond effectively. This lack of confidence can lead them to remain silent, even if they want to help.

4. **Believing Someone Else Will Act:** In a group setting, children might assume that someone else will help, leading to a diffusion of responsibility. This phenomenon is common in online environments where many people witness the same bullying incident, and everyone assumes that someone else will take action (Garfinkel, 2019).

Encouraging Children to Speak Up

Turning bystanders into upstanders requires a proactive approach from parents, educators, and communities. By fostering empathy, teaching communication skills, and modeling positive behavior, adults can help children build the confidence to stand up against cyberbullying.

1. **Fostering Empathy:** Teaching empathy is one of the most effective ways to encourage children to become upstanders. When children understand the emotional and psychological toll that cyberbullying takes on a victim, they are more likely to feel compelled to help (Gini et al., 2007).

2. **Discuss the Long-Term Impact of Bullying:** Help them understand that even "small" actions like liking a mean post or failing to defend someone can contribute to the victim's sense of isolation and sadness.

3. **Building Confidence in Conflict Resolution**: Many children hesitate to intervene because they don't know what to say or fear they'll make things worse. Parents can help by role-playing common scenarios and teaching their children conflict-resolution techniques.

4. **Teach Them How to Report Bullying**: Show your child how to report harmful content on social media platforms, apps, or games. Knowing how to report cyberbullying in a way that is safe and effective can empower them to take action without confrontation.

5. **Normalize Conversations About Standing Up:** Regularly discuss scenarios where your child might witness bullying and ask how they would respond. Encourage open dialogue about the importance of standing up for what's right, even when it's difficult.

6. **Share Stories of Upstanders:** Children often learn by example, so share stories of people who have stood up to bullies and made a positive impact. These examples can come from their own life, books, movies, or real-world news stories.

7. **Use positive reinforcement**: Acknowledge your child's courage when they speak up, and let them know that their actions make a difference. This recognition can boost their confidence and make them more likely to intervene in the future.

8. **Model upstanding behavior:** Children learn from the adults in their lives, so it's important to model the behavior you want them to adopt. If you witness bullying or unkind behavior, show your child how to address it constructively and compassionately.

9. **Creating a Safe Environment for Action**: Finally, ensure that your child feels safe when they choose to intervene. Let them know that they can always come to you or another trusted adult if they need help dealing with a cyberbullying situation.

10. **Encourage them to seek support:** Remind your child that they don't have to handle cyberbullying on their own. If they are unsure how to act or fear retaliation, they should feel comfortable seeking help from a trusted adult, whether a parent, teacher, or school counselor.

By empowering children to become upstanders instead of passive bystanders, we can help create a culture of kindness and accountability in the digital world. When children learn that they have the power to make a difference, they are more likely to intervene in cyberbullying situations and contribute to a safer, more supportive online community.

Part III: Preventing Cyberbullying

Chapter 7:
Teaching Digital Citizenship

As the internet becomes more deeply embedded in our lives, it's essential for children to learn not only how to navigate online spaces but also how to do so responsibly. Digital citizenship encompasses the skills and behaviors needed to engage safely, respectfully, and thoughtfully in the digital world. Teaching children digital citizenship is one of the most effective ways to prevent cyberbullying, helping them understand their roles and responsibilities online (Ribble, 2015).

In this chapter, we will explore digital citizenship, how parents can guide their children in setting healthy online boundaries, and the importance of instilling respect and empathy in their digital interactions.

What is Digital Citizenship?

Digital citizenship refers to the responsible and ethical use of technology and digital platforms. It involves understanding how to interact safely online, protecting personal information, respecting others, and contributing positively to online communities (Hollandsworth et al., 2017). At its core, digital citizenship is about teaching children that their online actions have real-world consequences.

For children growing up in a world where much of their social interactions take place online, learning digital citizenship is crucial. They must be aware of both their rights and responsibilities as participants in the digital world, which includes knowing how to protect themselves from harm and understanding how their behavior can impact others (Ribble & Bailey, 2007).

Teaching children digital citizenship encompasses a range of topics, such as:

1. **Privacy:** Children should learn how to protect their personal information and recognize the risks of oversharing.
2. **Safety:** They should understand how to identify potentially harmful interactions and know what to do when they encounter inappropriate content or behavior.
3. **Respect:** Just like in face-to-face interactions, children must treat others with kindness and consideration in digital spaces.

4. **Responsibility:** Kids should be mindful of their online footprint, understanding that what they post, share, and engage with can have lasting effects.

By emphasizing digital citizenship, parents can help prevent negative online behaviors like cyberbullying and foster a more supportive and positive digital environment for their children (Mihailidis & Thevenin, 2013).

Establishing Online Boundaries

One of the fundamental aspects of digital citizenship is the ability to set and maintain healthy boundaries in online spaces. Without clear boundaries, children may be exposed to harmful content, interacting with strangers, or sharing too much personal information.

Here are some key ways parents can help children establish online boundaries:

1. Control Who They Interact With

In online platforms, children must know that they don't have to interact with everyone who sends them a message or friend request. Parents should guide their children in understanding the importance of being selective about whom they engage with online.

- **Teach kids about friend requests and messages:** Encourage them only to accept friend requests or communicate with people they know in real life or who have been verified as safe by a trusted adult.
- **Monitor followers and friends lists:** Especially on social media, children can accumulate followers they don't know personally. Review their friend lists periodically to ensure they're interacting with people they trust (Kara et al., 2018).

2. **Setting Limits on What to Share**

One of the riskiest aspects of the internet is the ease with which personal information can be shared. Even something as simple as posting a photo or a status update can provide more information than intended.

- **Teach kids about oversharing:** Help children understand that once something is posted online, it's difficult to take it back. Emphasize that not all personal moments should be shared publicly, especially details about their location, school, or family.
- **Privacy settings:** Encourage children to use privacy settings to control who can see their posts, photos, and personal information on social media platforms.

Managing Time Spent Online

Setting boundaries isn't just about who they interact with or what they share—it also includes managing time. Excessive time online can increase exposure to negative behaviors like cyberbullying or harassment. Parents can help children set time limits to avoid spending too much time in online environments.

- **Set screen time limits:** Establishing reasonable daily limits for how long your child can use social media, messaging apps, or online games can help reduce the likelihood of harmful interactions and overexposure to negative content.
- **Encourage offline activities**: Make sure there is a balance between online and offline activities so children are not overly dependent on digital interactions for their social life and entertainment.

By teaching children how to establish and respect these online boundaries, parents can help protect them from potential harm and prevent situations that might lead to or escalate cyberbullying.

Respect and Empathy Online

A key component of digital citizenship is understanding that words and actions in online spaces can have the same emotional and psychological impact as in-person interactions. In the relatively anonymous environment of the internet, children may feel emboldened to say things they wouldn't say face-to-face. Teaching respect and empathy online is critical to preventing cyberbullying and creating a kinder, more supportive digital space.

1. Understanding the Impact of Words

It's important for children to realize that just because something happens online doesn't mean it's any less real or hurtful. Cyberbullying often occurs because people feel a disconnect between the virtual world and the real-world consequences of their actions. Teaching children that their words online can have a profound impact on someone's emotions and mental well-being is essential (Hinduja & Patchin, 2015).

- **Explain the emotional toll of online cruelty:** Help children understand how cyberbullying can lead to feelings of isolation, depression, and anxiety in victims. Encourage them to reflect on how they would feel if they were in the victim's position.

- **Discourage harmful humor:** Jokes, sarcasm, or teasing that may seem harmless to one person can be deeply hurtful to another. Teach children the importance of being mindful about their tone and the potential impact of their words.

2. Encouraging Empathy

Teaching empathy goes beyond simply avoiding hurtful behavior—it encourages children to actively think about the well-being of others. By fostering empathy, parents can help their children develop the skills to stand up against cyberbullying and contribute to positive online spaces.

- **Model empathy in online interactions:** Children learn by example, so parents need to model respectful and kind behavior online. Show them how to respond to negative comments with kindness or to ignore hurtful interactions.
- **Discuss the importance of kindness:** Talk to your children about how even small acts of kindness, like leaving a positive comment or reaching out to someone who seems down, can make a big difference in someone's online experience.

- **Encourage thoughtful engagement:** Teach your children to think before they post or comment. Ask them whether their words are necessary, kind, and helpful. Encourage them to pause and reflect on how their actions might make someone else feel.

Teaching digital citizenship provides children with the tools they need to navigate the complexities of the online world safely and responsibly. By establishing online boundaries and promoting respect and empathy, parents can play a critical role in preventing cyberbullying and fostering a more positive and supportive digital culture.

Chapter 8:
Family Rules for Online Safety

In today's digital age, online safety is one of the most pressing concerns for families. With children accessing the internet for entertainment, socializing, and education, it's vital for parents to establish clear guidelines that promote safety and healthy habits. By creating a family media agreement, monitoring online activity, and setting consequences for misuse, families can create an environment where children feel supported and protected while navigating the digital world (Miller, 2022).

In this chapter, we'll explore how parents can effectively set up family rules for online safety, offer strategies for monitoring children's online behavior, and provide guidance on what to do when those rules are broken.

Creating a Family Media Agreement

A family media agreement is a shared document or set of rules that outlines acceptable online behaviors, time limits, and privacy standards for everyone in the household (Kraft & Gollust, 2021). This agreement serves as a guide for children and parents to follow, helping ensure everyone is on the same page about expectations regarding digital use.

1. Collaborate on the Rules

Involving children in creating the agreement is essential. When kids help establish the rules, they're more likely to understand and respect them. Sit down as a family to discuss safe and responsible online behavior, and work together to create rules that make sense for your household.

- **Time limits**: Discuss how much time is appropriate for different online activities, such as gaming, social media, or schoolwork. It's important to balance screen time with outdoor play, reading, and family time.
- **Privacy rules:** Ensure children understand the importance of keeping personal information private. Establish clear guidelines about what is and isn't acceptable to share online, including photos, locations, and family details. Teach them the difference between private and public spaces online and how to navigate both safely.

2. Include the Whole Family

A family media agreement shouldn't just apply to children—it's important that parents and other caregivers also follow the rules. This sets a positive example for children and reinforces that online safety is a family responsibility. Parents should model good digital behavior, such as putting devices away during family meals, practicing respectful communication, and adhering to time limits.

3. Regular Review and Updates

As children grow older and technology evolves, the family media agreement should be updated. Make it a point to revisit the agreement periodically to adjust rules as needed. For example, what works for a seven-year-old's screen time might not be appropriate for a teenager who needs more online access for schoolwork or social interactions (Wright, 2022).

4. Sign the Agreement

To emphasize the importance of the agreement, have everyone in the family sign it. This formalizes the commitment to following the rules and shows that everyone has a shared responsibility for maintaining online safety.

Monitoring Online Activity

While it's essential to trust your children as they navigate the digital world, keeping an eye on their online activities is crucial for their safety. Monitoring your child's online interactions helps you catch potential issues early, such as exposure to inappropriate content, risky behaviors, or even cyberbullying (Livingstone et al., 2011). However, it's equally important to strike a balance between monitoring and respecting your child's privacy.

1. **Use Parental Controls**

Most devices and platforms have built-in parental controls that allow you to manage what content your children can access, set time limits, and even block certain websites. These controls can be useful for keeping your child safe, especially when they're younger.

- **Set content filters:** Use filters to block websites and apps that are inappropriate for your child's age group. These filters can help prevent exposure to violent, sexual, or otherwise harmful content.

- **Limit downloads and purchases:** Restrict your child's ability to download apps or make in-app purchases without your permission. This helps you stay aware of what new apps or games they're using.
- **Monitor communication**: Some parental controls allow you to see who your child communicates with online. This can help you spot red flags, like strangers trying to contact them.

2. Encourage Open Communication

The goal of monitoring isn't to spy on your child but to ensure they stay safe while giving them room to grow and learn. Open communication is key to building trust and ensuring your child feels comfortable coming to you with concerns.

- **Discuss their online activity regularly**: Make it a habit to ask your child about their favorite websites, games, or social media platforms. Show interest in what they're doing online so they feel more comfortable sharing.
- **Create a safe space for them to talk:** Let your children know they can come to you if they encounter something online that makes them uncomfortable. Reassure them that they won't be punished for being honest about their experiences.

- **Be transparent about monitoring:** It's important to be upfront with your child about the fact that you'll be monitoring their online activity. This helps them understand that your actions are motivated by concern for their safety rather than a lack of trust.

3. Look for Red Flags

Even with the best parental controls and open communication, it's still important to keep an eye out for signs that something may be wrong. Behavioral changes, like sudden anxiety around using devices or a reluctance to go online, can indicate your child is experiencing cyberbullying or other negative online interactions.

- **Sudden withdrawal:** If your child suddenly becomes secretive about their online activities or withdraws from family interactions, it could be a sign that they're dealing with online harassment or other issues.
- **Mood swings:** Unexplained mood changes, such as irritability, sadness, or anger after spending time online, may indicate your child is encountering problems on the internet.
- **Changes in online behavior:** If your child starts deleting messages, social media accounts, or browser

history frequently, it's worth having a conversation about what's going on.

Setting Consequences for Misuse

No matter how clear the rules are, there may come a time when they're broken. Establishing consequences for misuse of the internet is crucial to maintaining a safe and respectful online environment. It's important that these consequences are fair, clearly defined, and enforced consistently.

1. **Set Clear Expectations**

From the outset, ensure your children understand the consequences of breaking the family media agreement. Whether staying up past agreed-upon screen time limits or sharing personal information online, there should be clear consequences for violating the rules.

- **Immediate action for serious breaches**: If your child engages in dangerous behavior, such as communicating with strangers or sharing sensitive information, the consequences should be swift and significant. This might involve temporarily taking away device privileges or blocking certain apps.
- **Scaled consequences for minor breaches:** For less serious rule-breaking, like exceeding screen time limits or playing unapproved games, consider

consequences that fit the level of the breach. For instance, reduced screen time for a week could be an appropriate response.

2. Be Consistent

Consistency is key when it comes to enforcing consequences. If the rules are applied inconsistently, children may not take them seriously. Make sure that consequences are enforced each time a rule is broken so children understand the importance of following the guidelines.

3. Use Mistakes as Learning Opportunities

Rather than focusing solely on punishment, use rule-breaking as an opportunity for growth and learning. Discuss why the rule was broken and how your child can make better decisions in the future. This approach encourages reflection and reinforces the importance of online safety.

Creating a family media agreement, monitoring online behavior, and setting clear consequences are all essential steps in promoting online safety. These strategies empower children to use the internet responsibly while protecting them from potential dangers.

Chapter 9: Building Emotional Resilience and Teaching Kindness

In a world where children are constantly exposed to digital interactions, developing emotional resilience and practicing kindness are essential tools for navigating online and offline challenges. With the rise of cyberbullying, it's more important than ever to equip children with the emotional strength to recover from setbacks and the moral compass to treat others with kindness, even in the face of adversity.

This chapter will explore the concept of emotional resilience, the importance of teaching kindness, and how these qualities can not only protect children from the harmful effects of cyberbullying but also foster a positive, supportive digital environment. We'll also delve into practical strategies and activities parents can use to instill these values in their children.

What is Emotional Resilience?

Emotional resilience is the ability to bounce back from adversity, such as setbacks, challenges, or negative experiences. For children who are exposed to cyberbullying, emotional resilience becomes a critical factor in how well they can cope and recover from the psychological and emotional impacts of being targeted (Masten, 2001). When children develop emotional resilience, they learn to:

- **Process their emotions:** Rather than feeling overwhelmed or defeated, they understand how to acknowledge their emotions and work through them in a healthy way (Goleman, 1995).
- **Maintain perspective:** Resilient children can step back and view difficult situations in a broader context, realizing that setbacks or hurtful interactions don't define them (Luthar et al., 2000).
- **Adapt to change:** In the constantly shifting landscape of social interactions—especially online—emotionally resilient children are better equipped to handle sudden changes, disappointments, and stress (Werner & Smith, 2001).

Developing emotional resilience is essential not only in protecting against the harmful effects of cyberbullying but also in helping children grow into well-rounded, emotionally intelligent adults. By fostering emotional strength in children, we prepare them to navigate both the digital world and real life with confidence and grace.

Teaching Kindness: The Key to Positive Online and Offline Interactions

Kindness is a powerful antidote to negativity and bullying, both online and in real life. When children are taught to approach situations with kindness, they develop empathy, compassion, and the ability to build positive relationships with others. In digital spaces, where communication can often feel impersonal, kindness becomes even more critical (Blum et al., 2017).

- **Why Kindness Matters**

Kindness serves as a proactive approach to preventing bullying and creating a positive environment. When children learn to be kind to others, they are less likely to engage in harmful behaviors such as exclusion, teasing, or cyberbullying. In turn, this creates a ripple effect: kindness spreads, fostering a community where children feel safe, respected, and valued. By instilling values of kindness, parents can help prevent issues before they escalate. Teaching children to be kind not only protects them from becoming bullies themselves but also encourages them to become upstanders—individuals who speak out and act against bullying.

- **Empathy vs. Sympathy: Fostering Emotional Understanding**

It's essential to teach children the difference between empathy and sympathy. While sympathy involves feeling sorry for someone else's misfortune, empathy means truly understanding and sharing another person's feelings (Hoffman, 2000). Empathy allows children to see situations from another person's perspective, which can lead to more thoughtful, compassionate actions.

For example:

- Sympathy: "I feel bad for you."
- Empathy: "I understand why you're upset. I've felt that way too."

Empathy is a cornerstone of kindness. When children practice empathy, they are more likely to intervene in bullying situations, support their peers, and refrain from harmful behaviors. Parents can foster empathy in children by encouraging them to put themselves in someone else's shoes and think about how their words or actions might make others feel.

- **Practical Kindness Activities**

Teaching kindness requires more than just talking about it—it involves regular practice. Here are a few practical activities parents can use to help children embody kindness:

1. **Complimenting others online:** Encourage children to make positive comments on their friends' social media posts or to send supportive messages when someone shares an accomplishment.
2. **Kindness Challenge**: Set daily or weekly kindness goals, such as helping a classmate with homework, inviting someone to play a game, or simply offering a smile to someone who seems lonely.
3. **Role-playing scenarios:** Practice role-playing different situations where your child has the option to respond with kindness. For example, how would they react if they saw someone being cyberbullied? This activity helps children prepare for real-life situations.

- **Encouraging Kind Words and Actions**

Words have a powerful impact, especially in the digital world where tone and intent can easily be misinterpreted. Children need to understand that even seemingly harmless jokes or teasing can hurt others.

Parents can:

1. **Role-play with scenarios:** Help children practice responding to tricky situations with kind, constructive words. This could involve choosing kind responses when they witness an argument or learning how to de-escalate online conflicts.
2. **Model kindness:** Show children the power of kind words by modeling it yourself. Whether online or in person, use kind and thoughtful language in your interactions and explain the importance of being considerate.

The Ripple Effect of Kindness in Digital Spaces

In the vast and often impersonal world of the internet, small acts of kindness can have an outsized, lasting impact, especially within online communities. Just as a single drop of water can create ripples across a pond, simple gestures—like a compliment, a supportive comment, or even standing up for someone being mistreated—can send waves of positivity throughout digital spaces. These seemingly minor actions can change the tone of interactions, counter negativity, and make a significant difference in how others experience the online world (Polites et al., 2021).

- **How Kindness Makes a Difference**

In online communities, where anonymity often emboldens negative behavior, the power of kindness is profound. The internet, while offering incredible opportunities for connection and sharing, can also become a breeding ground for hostility, particularly through cyberbullying. This negativity often spreads rapidly, as people either participate or remain passive bystanders, further allowing harmful behavior to escalate (Smith et al., 2016). However, kindness has the unique ability to disrupt this cycle, creating a ripple effect that influences not just the direct recipients but the entire community.

For example:

1. **Combating Cyberbullying:** When children or adults respond to cyberbullying with kindness—whether by comforting the victim, reporting the incident, or standing up to the bully—they play an essential role in diffusing a potentially harmful situation. Instead of allowing negativity to take over, their actions can transform the interaction from

hostile to constructive. Standing up for someone being bullied not only helps the victim feel supported but also discourages the bully, showing that their actions will not go unchecked or unchallenged (Holt et al., 2016).

2. **Changing the Culture of Online Interactions:** Small acts of kindness can set the tone for entire online communities. If one child or individual leads by example by consistently choosing kind and respectful interactions, others are more likely to follow. This can create a ripple effect that fosters an overall culture of empathy and compassion. Over time, these actions contribute to a shift in the community's norms and values, encouraging more positive, uplifting behaviors (Wang et al., 2010).

3. **Building Trust and Belonging:** When kindness becomes a part of digital interactions, it fosters a sense of trust and belonging within the community. People feel safer to express themselves and engage with others without fear of judgment or harm. This sense of security and inclusion is crucial for both children and adults, especially those who may feel marginalized or vulnerable online (Barlett & Chamberland, 2018).

Parents can emphasize the importance of kindness by sharing real-life examples of children and individuals who have made a positive impact online. Stories of children who stood up to cyberbullies initiated positive online movements, or simply spread encouragement can serve as powerful teaching tools.

The beauty of kindness in digital spaces is that its effects often extend far beyond the initial act. A kind comment or supportive gesture can linger in the recipient's mind, helping to build their confidence and self-worth long after the interaction has passed. In communities, the ripple effect of one person's kindness can influence many, creating a culture of positivity that benefits everyone involved.

By teaching children that even the smallest acts of kindness can have a lasting impact, parents empower them to be agents of change in the digital world. In doing so, they help create a generation of digital citizens who understand the value of kindness and the powerful ripple effect it can have on others.

Developing Emotional Intelligence Through Kindness

Kindness and emotional intelligence are closely linked, as practicing kindness enhances a child's ability to understand and manage emotions. Emotional intelligence, which includes emotional awareness, empathy, and emotional regulation, plays a crucial role in fostering positive relationships and reducing harmful behaviors like cyberbullying (Goleman, 1995). When children learn to be kind, they are simultaneously developing the skills to navigate their own emotions and understand the feelings of others, both of which are essential for healthy online and offline interactions.

- **The Connection Between Kindness and Emotional Intelligence**

1. **Emotional Awareness:** Kindness begins with being aware of one's own emotions. Children who understand their feelings are more likely to notice how their actions, whether online or in person, can affect others. By recognizing their emotional state, they become better equipped to choose words and actions that reflect compassion rather than anger or frustration (Nolen-Hoeksema, 2001).

2. **Empathy:** One of the core elements of emotional intelligence is empathy, which is the ability to understand and share another person's feelings. Kindness stems from the ability to see situations from someone else's perspective. When children practice empathy, they can identify when someone might be hurt or upset and respond with care rather than contributing to negativity (Decety & Jackson, 2004).

3. **Emotional Regulation:** Emotional intelligence also involves learning how to manage one's emotions, particularly in challenging situations. Children who practice kindness are better able to regulate their emotions when they feel frustrated or angry. For instance, when faced with cyberbullying, a child with high emotional intelligence may pause, reflect on their feelings, and respond with empathy instead of escalating the situation (Gross, 2002).

- **Exercises to Build Emotional Awareness Through Kindness**

Parents can encourage the development of emotional intelligence through various activities that connect emotional awareness with kind behaviors. These exercises teach children how to be kind and build the emotional intelligence necessary to navigate complex social environments.

1. Discussing Feelings

Regularly ask your child how they're feeling and help them articulate those emotions. For example, if your child seems upset after an online interaction, ask questions like, "How did that comment make you feel?" This helps children become more aware of their emotional responses, which is the first step in managing them effectively (Mayer & Salovey, 1997). Encouraging children to express their feelings promotes open communication and emotional transparency, essential for healthy relationships.

2. Recognizing Emotional Triggers

Help your child recognize the situations that trigger strong emotions, such as feeling excluded from an online group or receiving a mean comment. Once they identify their emotional triggers, they can learn to pause and reflect before responding impulsively. Teaching children to take deep breaths or step away from the screen when they feel upset are useful emotional regulation strategies (Gross, 2002). This awareness can help them respond with kindness rather than frustration.

- **Managing Online Interactions**

Guide your child in managing their emotions during online interactions. For example, if they receive a hurtful message, encourage them to express their feelings to you first. Discuss how they can respond with kindness or choose not to engage in the negativity. This process teaches emotional self-control and the importance of responding thoughtfully rather than reacting impulsively (Holt et al., 2016).

By teaching children these key emotional intelligence skills, parents can help them not only to be kind but also to navigate the emotional complexities of digital interactions. Kindness, when paired with emotional intelligence, becomes a powerful tool for building positive, respectful online communities.

Building Kindness into Daily Habits

Kindness can be woven into the fabric of everyday life by making it a regular practice rather than a sporadic event. Families can help children develop the habit of kindness by incorporating simple, intentional acts into their daily routines.

1. **Daily Kindness Goals**

One effective way to make kindness a habit is to encourage children to set small, achievable kindness goals each day. These goals can be something as simple as sharing a positive comment online, helping a friend at school, or offering a compliment to someone. The key is to make these goals specific so children can easily integrate them into their day (Keltner et al., 2014).

2. **Reflect on Kindness**

Another powerful routine is to take time at the end of each day to reflect on acts of kindness. Families can gather at dinner or bedtime to discuss how each member contributed positively to someone else's day, either online or offline. This reflection helps reinforce the importance of kindness and allows children to see the ripple effect their actions can have on others (Peterson & Seligman, 2004).

By making kindness an intentional part of daily life, families can help children build lasting habits that promote empathy, emotional intelligence, and positive interactions in both digital and real-world environments.

Helping Children Cope: Fostering a Sense of Self-Worth

Building emotional resilience and practicing kindness are closely tied to a child's sense of self-worth. When children feel confident in themselves, they are more likely to approach situations with kindness and less likely to engage in negative behaviors like bullying (Schmidt et al., 2016).

- **Encouraging Problem-Solving Skills**

Teaching children how to approach conflicts with kindness, rather than anger or revenge, is a critical skill for maintaining healthy relationships. Help your child develop problem-solving skills by:

1. **Identifying the Problem:** Teach your child to identify what's bothering them in a conflict.
2. **Brainstorming Solutions:** Work with them to develop different ways to resolve the issue, emphasizing solutions that are kind and fair to everyone involved.

By developing problem-solving skills, children are more equipped to handle difficult situations with kindness and empathy (Snyder, 2000).

- **Fostering Self-Worth**

Children who feel good about themselves are more likely to treat others kindly and resist the temptation to engage in bullying behaviors. To help build your child's self-esteem:

1. **Celebrate Their Strengths:** Regularly praise your child for their unique qualities, accomplishments, and efforts, reinforcing their sense of self-worth.
2. **Encourage Positive Self-Talk:** Teach your child to replace negative thoughts with positive affirmations. For example, if they're feeling down, encourage them to focus on their strengths and what makes them special (Burns, 1980).

By building emotional resilience and teaching kindness, parents can equip their children with the tools they need to navigate the digital world with confidence and compassion. These qualities not only help children cope with challenges like cyberbullying but also empower them to create a more positive, supportive environment for others.

Part IV:

Responding to Cyberbullying

Chapter 10:

What to Do if Your Child is Cyberbullied

Cyberbullying is an incredibly challenging experience for any child to go through, and as a parent, it can feel overwhelming to know how to respond. When your child is being targeted online, it's essential to provide immediate support, take appropriate steps to stop the bullying and help your child recover emotionally. This chapter will guide you through the process of addressing cyberbullying, from talking to your child about the situation to documenting incidents and helping them heal from the emotional scars of the experience.

Talking to Your Child: Approaching the Conversation

The first and most important step in responding to cyberbullying is having a conversation with your child. This discussion needs to be approached with care, as your child may be feeling ashamed, embarrassed, or afraid to speak up. The goal is to create a safe space where they feel comfortable sharing their experience without fear of judgment or further distress.

1. **Approach the Conversation with Empathy and Patience**

When initiating the conversation, it's important to maintain a non-judgmental and calm demeanor. Cyberbullying can make a child feel vulnerable and defensive, so how you approach the situation will affect how open your child is about their experiences. Some tips include:

- **Listen first, speak second:** Begin by letting your child talk without interrupting or immediately offering solutions. Sometimes, all they need is to feel heard (Hinduja & Patchin, 2015).
- **Reassure your child:** Let them know that what they're going through is not their fault. Many children feel as though they are to blame for being bullied or

that they've done something to provoke it. Reassure them that they have your full support (Beran & Li, 2005).

- **Stay calm:** It's natural to feel anger or sadness when your child is being bullied, but showing too much emotion can make them more anxious. Try to stay calm and composed, showing them that you are their source of strength.

2. Ask Open-Ended Questions

Encourage your child to share more details about the cyberbullying by asking open-ended questions:

- "Can you tell me what's been happening online?"
- "How did it make you feel when you saw those messages?"
- "Has this been going on for a long time, or is this recent?"

These questions allow your child to express their feelings without feeling pressured to give short or defensive answers. By keeping the conversation open and supportive, you're more likely to get a fuller picture of what's happening (Kowalski et al., 2014).

Documenting and Reporting Cyberbullying

Once your child has shared the details of their experience, the next step is to take action to stop the bullying. Documentation and reporting are critical in dealing with cyberbullying effectively.

1. Collect Evidence

Encourage your child to save any messages, posts, or interactions that are harmful. This could include:

- **Screenshots of harmful messages:** Take screenshots of any messages or posts that are bullying your child. This serves as a record of what has been said and can be used as evidence if you need to report the incident (Finkelhor et al., 2014).
- **Dates and times of incidents:** Document when the bullying occurred. Keeping a timeline can help identify patterns or the frequency of the harassment.
- **Platforms involved:** Note where the bullying took place—whether on social media, through messaging apps, or in online games. Each platform has different reporting procedures, so knowing where the abuse occurred will help when you take further action.

2. Report the Cyberbullying

Once you've gathered the necessary evidence, you can report the behavior to the appropriate authorities. There are several channels through which you can report cyberbullying:

- **Report to the platform:** Most social media sites, messaging apps, and online gaming platforms have reporting mechanisms for harmful behavior. Use these tools to report the abuse and, in some cases, request the removal of harmful content.
- **Report to the school:** If the cyberbullying involves classmates, you may want to inform the school, especially if it's affecting your child's well-being or ability to focus in class. Schools often have policies in place to handle bullying, even if it occurs online (Wang et al., 2010).
- **Involve law enforcement if necessary:** If the bullying includes threats of physical harm or other serious behavior, it may be appropriate to contact law enforcement to ensure your child's safety.

The sooner you take steps to report the bullying, the faster it can be addressed and resolved. Reporting cyberbullying may deter the bully from continuing, as they will be aware that their actions are being monitored.

Helping Your Child Recover: Rebuilding Self-Esteem and Confidence

After the cyberbullying has been addressed, your child may still struggle with the emotional and psychological effects of the experience. It's important to help your child rebuild their confidence and sense of self-worth through various strategies that promote healing.

1. Reconnect with Positive Friendships

One of the most effective ways to help your child recover is to reconnect them with positive friendships and supportive social groups. Healthy friendships can act as a buffer against the negative impact of bullying and provide your child with a sense of belonging and support. Encourage your child to:

- **Spend time with friends:** Invite friends over for activities they enjoy, whether it's playing games, sports, or simply hanging out. Positive social interactions can boost your child's mood and remind them that they are valued.
- **Join supportive groups or clubs:** Consider encouraging your child to join a club or group that aligns with their interests. Whether it's a sports team, art class, or online community focused on shared

hobbies, being part of a supportive group can help restore their confidence.

2. Promote Positive Self-Image

Cyberbullying often targets a child's appearance, personality, or perceived weaknesses, which can deeply harm their self-esteem. To counteract these effects, parents can actively promote a positive self-image by:

- **Affirming your child's strengths:** Regularly highlight your child's unique talents, abilities, and positive qualities. Acknowledge their achievements and show that you value them for who they are.
- **Encouraging positive self-talk:** Teach your child to replace negative thoughts with positive affirmations. For example, if your child is feeling insecure about their appearance, encourage them to focus on the qualities they like about themselves.

3. Counseling and Professional Support

In some cases, cyberbullying can lead to lasting emotional scars that require professional intervention. If your child is struggling with feelings of sadness, anxiety, or depression that don't improve over time, seeking professional support may be necessary. Options include:

Therapy: A licensed therapist or counselor can help your child process their emotions and develop coping mechanisms to deal with the effects of cyberbullying (Willard, 2007).

Support groups: Some children find comfort in sharing their experiences with peers who have gone through similar challenges. Support groups provide a safe space for children to talk about their feelings and receive validation from others who understand what they're going through.

4. **Empowering Your Child Through Recovery**

Helping your child recover from cyberbullying involves more than addressing the bullying itself; it's about empowering them to regain their sense of self-worth and confidence. Here are a few final tips for supporting your child's recovery:

- **Encourage open communication:** Let your child know they can always come to you if they feel upset or need to talk. Keeping the lines of communication open ensures they won't feel alone in their struggles.

- **Help them develop problem-solving skills:** Work with your child to brainstorm strategies for handling future challenges constructively. This could include ignoring mean comments, blocking harmful users, or seeking support when needed.
- **Reinforce their resilience:** Remind your child that they are strong and capable of overcoming adversity. Celebrate their progress and resilience as they work through the emotional effects of cyberbullying.

In helping your child recover from cyberbullying, the ultimate goal is to build their resilience, restore their confidence, and foster a sense of emotional well-being that will protect them from future challenges.

Chapter 11:

Addressing Cyberbullying if Your Child is the Bully

Discovering that your child is engaging in cyberbullying can be distressing and overwhelming. No parent wants to imagine their child harming others, especially in such a pervasive way. However, if your child is involved in cyberbullying, it's crucial to address the behavior early and effectively. This chapter will guide you through how to confront the situation, teach empathy and responsibility, and ensure that your child understands the impact of their actions.

Confronting the Behavior: How to Approach the Situation

The first step in addressing cyberbullying behavior is having a conversation with your child. This discussion should be approached carefully to avoid escalating tensions or causing your child to shut down. The goal is to help your child understand the seriousness of their actions while providing a path toward better behavior.

1. **Stay Calm and Avoid the Blame**

Finding out your child is bullying others can trigger strong emotions like anger, disappointment, or frustration. However, reacting too harshly or immediately blaming your child can make them defensive or unwilling to open up. Instead:

- **Stay calm:** Take a deep breath and approach the conversation calmly. Your child is more likely to listen and engage if they don't feel attacked (Feng et al., 2018).
- **Avoid labeling your child:** Saying things like "You're a bully" can create shame and make them feel defined by their mistakes. Instead, focus on the behavior, not their identity, by saying, "I've noticed you've been involved in some hurtful behavior online" (Lange, 2020).

2. **Use Open-Ended Questions**

Instead of confronting your child with accusations, encourage a dialogue by asking open-ended questions. These questions help you understand your child's perspective and give them a chance to explain their actions. Some examples include:

- "Can you help me understand what's been happening online?"
- "How do you feel when you send those messages or post those comments?"
- "Do you think what you're doing might be hurting someone?"

By asking these types of questions, you give your child an opportunity to reflect on their behavior and consider the impact of their actions. This also helps you gauge whether your child fully understands what they've done and why it's harmful (O'Reilly & Dogra, 2020).

3. Set Clear Boundaries and Consequences

Once you've had a conversation with your child, it's important to establish boundaries around their online behavior and set clear consequences if those boundaries are crossed. This includes:

- **Limiting online access:** If your child has been using certain platforms or messaging apps to engage in bullying, consider restricting their access until they demonstrate more responsible behavior.
- **Establishing consequences:** Be upfront about what will happen if the behavior continues. For example, explain that if they engage in cyberbullying

again, they may lose access to certain devices or platforms.

Ensure that the consequences are fair and proportionate to the behavior but also firm enough to convey the seriousness of the situation. Your child must understand there are real consequences for harmful behavior (Kowert, 2020).

Teaching Empathy and Responsibility

One of the most effective ways to address bullying behavior is by teaching your child empathy and helping them take responsibility for their actions. Cyberbullying often stems from a lack of understanding or consideration for how online words and actions can impact others. Here's how you can help your child develop empathy and a sense of accountability.

1. **Encourage Your Child to Reflect on Their Actions**

A key step in building empathy is encouraging your child to put themselves in the shoes of those they've harmed. Ask your child to reflect on how their words and actions might feel if they were on the receiving end. Some questions you can ask include:

- "How do you think the person you bullied feels right now?"
- "What would it be like if someone said those things to you?"
- "Do you think you would want to continue using that platform if you were being treated that way?"

These questions help your child develop emotional awareness and understand the real-world impact of their behavior (Davis, 2018). You can also ask them to imagine what kind of environment they want to create online. This reflection process can guide your child toward more positive and respectful interactions.

2. Discuss the Consequences of Cyberbullying

It's essential to educate your child about the long-term consequences of cyberbullying, not only for the victim but also for the bully. Explain that their actions can have lasting effects on others' mental health and well-being and that in some cases, cyberbullying can even lead to serious legal consequences. Make sure they understand that cyberbullying is not a harmless activity or "just a joke" but something that can deeply harm others (Hinduja & Patchin, 2015).

You can also discuss the importance of building positive online communities and how their behavior contributes to the overall environment of the digital spaces they inhabit.

3. Teach Responsibility and Restorative Actions

Teaching your child to take responsibility for their actions is a critical part of addressing cyberbullying. This involves helping them understand the need to repair relationships and make amends for the harm they've caused.

Here's how you can guide your child toward taking responsibility:

- **Apologizing:** Encourage your child to offer a genuine apology to the person they've bullied. This might involve writing a message or, if appropriate, speaking directly to the person. Make sure your child understands that the apology should be sincere and reflect their understanding of the harm they've caused.
-
- **Repairing the harm**: Depending on the situation, your child might need to take additional steps to make amends. For example, if they've posted hurtful comments publicly, they could post a follow-up message retracting their hurtful words and expressing

regret. Encourage your child to think about ways they can contribute positively to the environment where the bullying took place.

While it can be difficult for children to admit they were wrong, taking responsibility and working to repair relationships is a vital part of their development. It also teaches them that while mistakes happen, they have the power to make things right.

Cultivating Empathy and Kindness at Home

Building empathy and teaching kindness starts at home. As parents, you can set the tone for respectful and empathetic behavior both online and offline. Here are some ways to reinforce these values in your child's daily life.

1. Model Kindness and Empathy

Children often learn how to treat others by observing the adults around them. Be a role model for empathy and kindness by treating others with respect, especially in situations where conflict or disagreement arises. Show your child how to navigate disagreements with compassion and how to resolve conflicts without resorting to hurtful words or actions (Berkowitz & Bier, 2016).

2. Engage in Empathy-Building Activities

Consider engaging your child in activities that build empathy, such as:

- **Volunteering:** Participating in community service or volunteering together can help your child understand the importance of helping others and being kind to those in need.
- **Discussing emotions:** Encourage your child to discuss their feelings and ask how others might feel in various situations. Discussing emotions openly can help your child become more aware of how their actions affect others.

Reading stories about kindness: Reading books or watching movies that emphasize themes of kindness, empathy, and understanding can help your child internalize these values.

3. Encourage Positive Online Behavior

Finally, reinforce the idea that kindness and empathy should extend to online spaces. Remind your child that behind every username or profile picture is a real person with real feelings. Encourage them to think carefully before they post or send messages and to always choose kindness in their online interactions (O'Reilly & Dogra, 2020).

Addressing cyberbullying when your child is the bully is not an easy task, but it's an important opportunity for growth. With your guidance, your child can learn from their mistakes, develop empathy, and become a more responsible digital citizen. The goal is not just to stop the behavior but to help your child become someone who contributes positively to their online and offline communities.

Chapter 12:

How to Create a Safe and Open Online Environment at Home

In today's digital world, creating a safe and open online environment at home is essential to protecting your children from cyberbullying and helping them navigate the complexities of the internet. The key to building this environment lies in open communication, trust, and empowering your child to make smart decisions online. In this chapter, we'll explore how to establish a judgment-free zone, build trust, hold regular family check-ins, and empower your child to take control of their online safety.

Creating a Judgment-Free Zone

One of the most important things you can do as a parent is to establish a judgment-free space where your child feels comfortable discussing their online experiences without fear of punishment or harsh judgment. Cyberbullying, inappropriate content, or uncomfortable interactions can happen to any child, and they need to feel safe coming to you for help (Hinduja & Patchin, 2015).

1. **Encourage Open Communication**

To create a judgment-free zone, you must foster an atmosphere of open communication. Start by making it clear to your child that they can talk to you about anything they encounter online—whether it's positive or negative—without fear of immediate consequences like losing their internet privileges. The more open your child feels, the more likely they will be to seek your guidance when they face challenges online (Kowert, 2020).

Here's how to encourage that openness:

- **Listen without interrupting:** When your child shares something about their online experiences, resist the urge to jump in with advice or solutions immediately. Let them express their thoughts and feelings first.
- **Avoid overreacting:** If your child reveals something upsetting, such as being bullied online, remain calm. Overreacting could make them hesitant to approach you in the future.
- **Acknowledge their feelings:** Validating your child's emotions is crucial. Even if what they're experiencing doesn't seem severe to you, it might feel overwhelming to them. Show empathy and understanding before offering guidance (Gorzig, 2021).

2. Remove Fear of Consequences

Many children fear that if they tell their parents about cyberbullying or an inappropriate online encounter, they'll lose their devices or online access. While boundaries are important, it's crucial to strike a balance between setting rules and creating an environment where your child feels safe sharing their experiences (Livingstone et al., 2011). Instead of jumping to consequences like restricting device use, focus on solutions and working together to address the situation.

Building Trust with Your Child

Trust is the foundation of any healthy relationship, including the one you share with your child. When it comes to navigating the online world, your child needs to know they can trust you to help them make good decisions and support them when challenges arise (Simmons, 2020). Building trust takes time, but it is essential for ensuring your child feels comfortable turning to you for help.

1. Foster a Collaborative Relationship

A great way to build trust is to take a collaborative approach to your child's online activities. Instead of enforcing strict rules without explanation, involve your child in discussions about their online behavior, privacy settings, and safety measures. Ask for their input and make decisions together. This collaborative approach makes your child feel respected and valued, which, in turn, strengthens trust.

2. Be Consistent and Fair

Consistency is key to building trust. If you set certain rules or expectations for your child's online behavior, make sure you enforce them consistently but fairly. Avoid changing the rules suddenly or imposing severe consequences without warning. Being consistent shows your child that they can rely on you to be fair and reasonable.

3. Share Your Own Online Experiences

Another way to build trust is to share your own experiences with the digital world. Let your child know that you understand the challenges of online interactions because you've experienced them, too. Whether it's dealing with difficult people, navigating social media, or maintaining privacy, sharing your personal insights can create a sense of solidarity and understanding between you and your child.

Regular Family Check-ins

Establishing regular family check-ins is an effective way to create an ongoing dialogue about online behavior and experiences. These meetings provide a structured opportunity for your child to share their thoughts, ask questions, and express concerns. They also allow you to stay informed about your child's online activities and any challenges they may be facing (Wong et al., 2020).

1. **Setting Up Family Meetings**

You can start by scheduling regular family meetings, whether they're weekly or biweekly, to discuss what's happening in your child's online world. Here's how to structure these check-ins:

- **Keep it casual:** Avoid making the meetings feel like formal or disciplinary sessions. The more relaxed the atmosphere, the more likely your child will be to open up.
- **Focus on sharing:** Encourage everyone in the family to share their online experiences, from the fun and positive to the challenging and concerning.
- **Discuss digital habits:** Use these meetings as an opportunity to discuss healthy digital habits, such as setting screen time limits, being respectful online, and practicing digital citizenship.

2. **Address Online Challenges Together**

Family check-ins provide an opportunity to address online challenges as a team. If your child is experiencing cyberbullying, encountering inappropriate content, or facing other difficulties, these meetings give you the chance to offer guidance and work together on solutions. It also reinforces the idea that they are not alone in dealing with these issues.

Empowering Your Child to Make Safe Choices

Ultimately, your goal as a parent is to empower your child to take control of their online safety. By teaching them how to assess risks, make informed decisions, and respond to challenges, you help them develop the confidence to navigate the digital world responsibly.

1. **Teach Risk Assessment**

One of the most valuable skills you can teach your child is how to assess risks online. This includes recognizing potentially harmful situations, such as interacting with strangers, sharing personal information, or engaging in negative online behavior. Encourage your child to ask themselves the following questions before making decisions online:

- Is this information safe to share? Teach your child the importance of protecting personal information like their full name, address, and school name.
- Do I know this person well enough to interact with them? Encourage your child to only interact with people they know and trust.
- Could my actions hurt someone else? Help your child think critically about how their words and actions online might affect others.

2. Encourage Independence with Guidance

While it's important to set boundaries and monitor your child's online activity, it's equally important to give them some independence. Empowering your child to make their own decisions, with your guidance, helps build their confidence and critical thinking skills. Gradually increase their level of responsibility as they demonstrate good judgment and responsible behavior online.

3. Reinforce Smart Online Behavior

Praise your child when they make smart decisions online, such as avoiding risky interactions, reporting inappropriate content, or standing up for someone being bullied. Positive reinforcement not only builds your child's confidence but also encourages them to continue making safe and responsible choices.

Creating a safe and open online environment at home is a shared responsibility between you and your child. By fostering open communication, building trust, holding regular check-ins, and empowering your child to make safe choices, you create a foundation for navigating the digital world together. The goal is not only to protect your child from cyberbullying and online dangers but also to help them develop the skills they need to thrive in an increasingly connected world.

Chapter 13:

Cyberbullying in the Era of Emerging AI

As technology advances, artificial intelligence (AI) is transforming how we interact online. While AI offers incredible possibilities, it also introduces new risks for young people. Cyberbullying has evolved with these changes, leveraging AI to increase its reach, intensity, and complexity. This chapter explores the ways AI influences cyberbullying and how parents can help protect their children from these new forms of digital harm.

AI-Enhanced Cyberbullying Tactics

AI tools have become powerful instruments for those with harmful intentions, allowing bullies to automate, amplify, and anonymize their actions in ways that were not possible before. Here are some examples:

- **Deepfake Content**: AI can create "deepfakes"—fake images, videos, or audio recordings that look or sound like real people. These can be used to humiliate or harass a child by making it appear as if they are saying or doing something embarrassing. Deepfakes are challenging because they can spread quickly, often becoming viral before they are proven fake.

- **Automated Harassment**: Some bullies now use AI-powered chatbots to send harmful messages continuously, making it harder for victims to block or avoid these attacks. The ability to automate harassment enables bullies to maintain a constant online presence without being directly involved.

- **Manipulated Images and Fake Profiles**: AI tools make it easy to create fake images or profiles. Bullies can quickly edit photos, adding a person's likeness to embarrassing situations, or set up fake social media accounts pretending to be the victim, leading to misunderstandings or harm to their reputation.

Parents should be aware of these emerging tactics and talk openly with their children about how to recognize and handle AI-generated content that could be used maliciously.

Impact of AI on Privacy and Cybersecurity

The vast reach of AI has made it easier to gather and use personal information, which can be exploited by cyberbullies. Here are some privacy and security risks that are especially relevant:

- **Data Mining and Profiling**: AI can process vast amounts of information, such as social media activity, photos, and even location data. This allows bullies to use AI-generated profiles of their targets, identifying what might make them vulnerable. Children should be educated about privacy settings and careful with the information they share online.

- **Location Tracking and Doxing Risks**: Many AI-driven apps request access to location data, potentially exposing children to risks if this information is misused. "Doxing," the act of sharing someone's personal information publicly, can be amplified by AI, making it easy to spread sensitive information widely.

Parents can support their children by explaining the importance of privacy settings, limiting location-sharing features, and encouraging thoughtful decisions about what they share online.

AI and Parental Controls

AI has also provided new tools for parents to monitor online behavior and detect signs of distress or bullying. However, AI-powered parental controls have limitations and are not a substitute for open communication.

AI-Powered Monitoring Tools: Many parental control apps now use AI to detect suspicious content in children's messages, emails, or social media posts. For example, AI can flag certain keywords or unusual patterns of communication that might suggest bullying, harassment, or risky behavior. These tools are a good resource for detecting early warning signs.

Limitations of AI in Cyberbullying Detection:

AI cannot always understand the context, sarcasm, or subtle nuances in messages. An innocent message or joke might be flagged as harmful, while some harmful behaviors can go undetected if they're not directly abusive. Relying solely on AI may give parents a false sense of security, so it's essential to also keep lines of communication open with children.

Parents should view AI as a supplement to, rather than a replacement for, family discussions about online safety. Checking in regularly and fostering a supportive environment encourages children to report concerns without fear of judgment or punishment.

Empowering Children with AI Literacy

With AI continuing to evolve, it's essential that children are prepared to recognize and respond to these new risks. Teaching children about AI and its potential effects on their online experiences is crucial.

- **Teaching Children About AI**: Help children understand what AI is, how it works, and how it can be used both positively and negatively. Knowing that some online content is AI-generated will make them more critical viewers, reducing the risk of being misled or manipulated by digital media.

- **Developing Critical Thinking Skills**: Encourage children to question the authenticity of what they see online. Simple reminders, like "Is this source trustworthy?" or "Does this seem like something the person would actually say?" can help them recognize manipulated content or deepfakes.

- **Promoting Verification Skills**: Encourage children to verify information before sharing it. Teaching them to cross-check facts, use reverse image searches, and think twice before engaging with suspicious content can be empowering tools in their digital toolkit.

By helping children develop AI literacy, parents prepare them to recognize AI-generated threats and respond to them with confidence and caution.

Practical Tips for Parents

- **Stay Informed**: As AI technology evolves, it's essential to stay updated on new trends and potential risks. Knowing about deepfakes, bots, and privacy issues can help you guide your child through these complex topics.

- **Set Boundaries and Limits on AI-Enabled Apps**: Limit or monitor your child's use of AI-driven apps or features, especially those that track location or access personal data. Encourage them to use these tools responsibly and discuss potential risks.

- **Maintain Open Communication**: Encourage your child to discuss any confusing or uncomfortable experiences online. Let them know that they can come to you if they encounter AI-manipulated content, such as deepfakes or bots, or if they suspect they are being targeted by automated messages.

As AI continues to transform the digital landscape, cyberbullying will evolve alongside it. By understanding these new AI-driven risks, parents can equip themselves and their children to face these challenges. Staying informed, fostering open communication, and encouraging AI literacy are key steps in helping children safely navigate this increasingly complex digital world. With the right support and resources, children can learn to protect themselves from these new forms of cyberbullying and use AI to their advantage as responsible digital citizens.

Conclusion:

Navigating the Future of Cyberbullying

As we move further into a digital world, the challenges that come with it, particularly cyberbullying, continue to evolve. For parents, the key to navigating these challenges lies in staying informed, vigilant, and proactive. The online landscape shifts rapidly, and with it, the tools and methods of bullying transform. However, by equipping yourself with knowledge, building an open relationship with your child, and creating a supportive home environment, you can help your children thrive online and in life.

The Importance of Staying Informed

The digital world is constantly changing, with new platforms, trends, and communication tools emerging every day. For parents, staying informed is one of the most important steps in safeguarding your child from cyberbullying and other online dangers. Being aware of the latest trends in social media, messaging apps, and online games can help you better understand the spaces your child is navigating and recognize potential risks (Hinduja & Patchin, 2015).

1. **Keeping Up with Social Media Trends**

Today's children and teens are often early adopters of new platforms. What's popular today may be replaced by a new app tomorrow. To keep pace with the rapidly evolving social media landscape, parents should:

- **Research new apps and platforms:** When your child mentions a new platform or game, take the time to learn about it. Many websites and parent groups offer reviews and safety ratings for apps commonly used by kids (Anderson & Jiang, 2018).
- **Familiarize yourself with platform features:** Each social media platform has different privacy settings, reporting tools, and communication methods. Understanding how these features work can help you guide your child in setting up safe profiles and navigating online spaces responsibly (Hinduja & Patchin, 2015).
- **Engage with online communities:** Join parent forums or social media groups focused on online safety. These communities are great resources for staying updated on the latest cyberbullying trends, security concerns, and preventative measures.

2. Recognizing Evolving Forms of Cyberbullying

As technology advances, so do the tactics used by bullies. Parents need to recognize that cyberbullying is not confined to traditional forms such as hurtful comments or exclusion. The following trends highlight the evolving nature of online harassment:

- **Anonymous apps**: Many new apps allow users to post comments or send messages anonymously, making it easier for bullies to target others without consequences (Kowalski et al., 2014).
- **Deepfakes and manipulated images:** Technology now allows for the creation of realistic but false images and videos, which can be used to spread harmful rumors or humiliate individuals.
- **Group bullying:** Cyberbullying often involves groups of peers who gang up on a target through group chats, forums, or comment sections, making it harder for victims to defend themselves.

By staying aware of these trends, you can help your child recognize and report cyberbullying when it happens and guide them on how to avoid engaging in or encouraging such behavior.

Final Thoughts: Helping Your Child Navigate the Digital World

As a parent, you hold the power to help your child develop the tools they need to navigate the digital world safely and confidently. While cyberbullying is a serious concern, it is not insurmountable. By staying informed, fostering open communication, and equipping your child with emotional resilience, you can create a protective and supportive environment where they can thrive.

1. Raising Awareness

Awareness is the first step in combating cyberbullying. By understanding the various forms of cyberbullying, recognizing the warning signs, and knowing where it most commonly takes place, you are better equipped to prevent or address it in its early stages. When children understand what cyberbullying looks like, they are more likely to avoid engaging in harmful behavior themselves and to stand up for others who are being targeted (Anderson & Jiang, 2018).

2. Prevention Strategies

Prevention is the cornerstone of protecting your child from cyberbullying. Teaching digital citizenship, establishing family media agreements, and setting clear consequences for online misuse are all essential parts of prevention. By providing your child with the tools to behave respectfully and responsibly online, you reduce the likelihood of them becoming involved in cyberbullying, either as a victim or a perpetrator (Kowalski et al., 2014).

Additionally, fostering kindness and empathy within your family is one of the most effective ways to counteract the negativity that fuels cyberbullying. When children understand the value of kindness and develop empathy for others, they are less likely to engage in harmful behavior and more likely to become upstanders who help protect their peers from bullying.

3. Providing Support

Despite your best efforts, your child may still encounter cyberbullying at some point. In those moments, your role as a supportive, understanding, and proactive parent becomes crucial. Children who feel supported by their families are more likely to recover from the emotional impact of bullying and regain their self-esteem.

Encouraging open dialogue, seeking professional help when necessary, and providing opportunities for positive social connections can help your child rebuild their confidence and move (Hinduja & Patchin, 2015).

Resources for Parents and Children

Here are some valuable resources to help parents and children combat cyberbullying, promote digital safety, and foster emotional resilience:

1. **Common Sense Media**: Provides reviews, ratings, and advice on apps, games, and social media platforms. A great resource for parents looking to understand the digital world their children inhabit.

2. **StopBullying.gov:** Offers comprehensive resources for parents, educators, and children on recognizing, preventing, and responding to bullying, including cyberbullying.

3. **ConnectSafely:** A nonprofit organization dedicated to educating users about online safety, privacy, and security. It provides guides on popular social media platforms and advice on how to protect children online.

4. **The CyberSmile Foundation:** A charity that offers support to victims of cyberbullying and online abuse. They provide resources for coping with cyberbullying and tools for building positive online communities.\

5. **National Center for Missing & Exploited Children**: Provides information on protecting children from online predators, as well as resources for reporting cyberbullying and other forms of online abuse.

The digital world can be daunting, but with the right knowledge, support, and strategies in place, parents can help their children navigate it safely. Cyberbullying may continue to evolve, but so will the tools and approaches we use to combat it. By staying informed, fostering kindness and empathy, and creating open lines of communication with your child, you can ensure that they grow up as responsible, resilient digital citizens.

Appendix:
Sample Family Media Agreement

This agreement is structured to create a balanced approach to technology, reinforce positive behavior, and encourage open conversations about online safety:

We, the _____ (Family Name) family, agree to work together to create a safe, balanced, and respectful online environment. By following these guidelines, we aim to protect ourselves and each other from the risks of online interactions, such as cyberbullying, and to ensure healthy digital habits.

1. Screen Time Limits

- **Weekdays**: No more than _____ (no. of hours) of screen time per day, with a focus on schoolwork and educational content.
- **Weekends**: A maximum of _____ (no. of hours) of recreational screen time.
- **Family time**: No screens during meals, family activities, or one hour before bedtime.

2. Privacy Rules

- Keep personal information private. Do not share your full name, address, school name, or other identifying details online.
- Avoid sharing photos, videos, or posts without the consent of those involved.
- Use privacy settings on all social media accounts and apps.

3. Kindness and Respect Online

- Treat others the way you would like to be treated. Use kind words and actions in all online interactions.
- If you see someone being bullied or harassed, stand up for them, report it, or seek help from a trusted adult.
- Avoid posting negative, hurtful, or inappropriate comments.

4. Cyberbullying

- We will not participate in any form of cyberbullying, including harassment, exclusion, or spreading rumors.

- If you are experiencing or witnessing cyberbullying, report it immediately to a parent or trusted adult.

5. Approved Apps and Websites

- Only use apps and websites approved by parents.
- Download new apps or games only with parental permission.
- Avoid interacting with strangers or people you don't know in real life.

6. Monitoring and Safety

- Parents may check online activity and conversations to ensure safety.
- Use parental controls to block inappropriate content and limit screen time.
- Report any suspicious or uncomfortable interactions to a parent immediately.

7. Consequences for Breaking the Rules

- Violations of this agreement will result in _____ _____ _____[agreed-upon consequence, e.g., loss of screen time for [x days], no gaming for a week, etc.].
- We will review and adjust this agreement as needed.

Signatures

Parent(s): _____

Child(ren):

_____
_____
_____
_____

_____

Date: _____

Glossary:

AI (Artificial Intelligence): Computer systems designed to mimic human intelligence and decision-making, increasingly used in platforms kids interact with, such as social media, games, and chatbots.

Anonymity: The ability to hide one's real identity online, which can sometimes encourage people (including children) to use language or behavior they wouldn't in face-to-face settings.

Boundaries: Clear rules and limits set by parents or caregivers around language use and behavior online, helping children understand what's acceptable.

Casual Swearing: Mild or everyday swearing (e.g., "damn," "hell") used without intent to harm, often seen in gaming chats or social media.

Cyberbullying: The use of digital communication to intimidate, harass, or insult others, sometimes involving profane or abusive language.

Digital Footprint: The trail of data and content left by a person's online activities, including posts, comments, and language use, which can have lasting reputational effects.

Emotional Regulation: The ability to manage and control emotional responses, an important skill for children to develop instead of venting through swearing.

Empathy: The capacity to understand and share the feelings of others, crucial in teaching children to consider the impact of their words online.

Gaming Culture: The social norms, behaviors, and language common in online gaming environments, often including swearing as part of competitive or emotional expression.

Harmful Swearing: Offensive language intended to insult, belittle, or hurt others, which can escalate into bullying or harassment.

Monitoring Tools: Software or apps used by parents to oversee their children's online activities, helping manage exposure to inappropriate language and interactions.

Parental Controls: Settings on devices or apps that limit what content children can access or who they can communicate with, helping prevent exposure to swearing and harmful language.

Peer Pressure: The influence of friends or online communities that can push children to adopt certain behaviors, including swearing, to fit in.

Privacy Settings: Options on social media or apps that control who can see or interact with a user's content, helping protect children from unwanted exposure.

Respectful Communication: The practice of using kind, thoughtful, and non-hurtful language, both online and offline.

Role-Playing: A teaching strategy where children practice appropriate responses to online challenges, such as encountering swearing, by acting out scenarios.

Social Media: Digital platforms like TikTok, Instagram, and YouTube where children interact with peers and are often exposed to trends, including swearing.

Swearing Challenge (e.g., TikTok "Cursing Challenge"): Online trends or viral activities that encourage the use of swear words for entertainment or social approval.

Viral Trends: Rapidly spreading online challenges or behaviors, sometimes involving swearing, that children may encounter or imitate.

References

Anderson, M., & Jiang, J. (2018). Teens, Social Media & Technology 2018. Pew Research Center. https://www.pewresearch.org/internet/2018/05/31/teens-social-media-technology-2018/

Archer, J., & Coyne, S. M. (2005). An integrated review of indirect, relational, and social aggression. Personality and Social Psychology Review, 9(3), 212-230.

Baldry, A. C., & Farrington, D. P. (2000). Bullies and victims in school: A review of the literature. Aggression and Violent Behavior, 5(2), 117-130.

Barlett, C. P., & Chamberland, L. (2018). The impact of kindness on cyberbullying: Evidence from a longitudinal study. Journal of Adolescence, 68, 1-10.

Berkowitz, M. W., & Bier, M. C. (2016). What Works in Character Education: A Research-Driven Guide for Educators. The Character Education Partnership.

Beran, T., & Li, Q. (2005). Cyberbullying: The nature and extent of the problem. Canadian Journal of School Psychology, 20(2), 82-100.

Blum, R. W., Beuhring, T., & Shew, M. (2017). Protecting teens from bullying: A guide for parents and educators. The Journal of Adolescent Health, 60(2), 120-125.

Burns, D. D. (1980). Feeling Good: The New Mood Therapy. William Morrow.

Campbell, M. A., Spears, B., Slee, P., Butler, D., & Kift, S. (2018). Victims' perceptions of traditional and cyberbullying, and the psychosocial correlates of their victimization. Emotional and Behavioural Difficulties, 13(3), 389-402.

Cassidy, W., Faucher, C., & Jackson, M. (2013). Cyberbullying among youth: A comprehensive review of current literature and its implications for research and policy. Springer.

Decety, J., & Jackson, P. L. (2004). The functional architecture of the human empathy system: Inference and criticism. Trends in Cognitive Sciences, 8(10), 471-478.

Davis, K. (2018). Building Empathy in Children: Strategies for Parents and Educators. Child Psychology Journal, 22(4), 345-359.

Feng, J., Zhai, Z., & Zhang, L. (2018). Parental Guidance and Children's Cyberbullying: An Empirical Study. Computers in Human Behavior, 88, 191-199.

Finkelhor, D., Jones, L. M., & Wong, J. (2014). Trends in youth victimization: A report from the

National Survey of Children's Exposure to Violence. Office of Juvenile Justice and Delinquency Prevention.

Garfinkel, H. (2019). Diffusion of responsibility: Understanding bystander behavior. Journal of Social Issues, 75(4), 991-1006.

Gini, G., Pozzoli, T., & Hymel, S. (2007). Individual and contextual correlates of bullying and victimization in children and adolescents. International Journal of Behavioral Development, 31(6), 546-559.

Goleman, D. (1995). Emotional Intelligence: Why it can matter more than IQ. Bantam Books.

Gorzig, A. (2021). Children's online safety: Perspectives and challenges. In K. McGhee (Ed.), Cyberbullying and online behavior (pp. 67-82). Springer.

Gross, J. J. (2002). Emotion regulation: Affective, cognitive, and social consequences. Psychophysiology, 39(3), 281-291.

Hamm, M. P., Newton, A. S., Chisholm, A., Shulhan, J., Milne, A., Sundar, P., Ennis, H., Scott, S. D., & Hartling, L. (2015). Prevalence and effect of cyberbullying on children and young people: A scoping review of social media studies. JAMA Pediatrics, 169(8), 770-777.

Hinduja, S., & Patchin, J. W. (2015). Bullying beyond the schoolyard: Preventing and responding to cyberbullying. Corwin Press.

Hoffman, M. L. (2000). Empathy and moral development: Implications for caring and justice. Cambridge University Press.

Hollandsworth, D., Dowdy, L., & Donovan, A. (2017). Digital citizenship in K–12: The role of school counselors. Journal of School Counseling, 15(7), 1-24.

Holt, M. K., Priel, M. R., & Topping, K. J. (2016). Bystander behavior in cyberbullying: The impact of the bystander's role on the victim's experience. Cyberpsychology, Behavior, and Social Networking, 19(5), 302-307.

Huang, Y., & Chou, C. (2010). The impact of cyberbullying on children's emotional and behavioral adjustments. Journal of School Violence, 9(3), 272-285.

Kara, E., Akçay, A., & Toprak, M. (2018). The role of parental supervision in adolescent internet use. International Journal of Cyber Behavior, Psychology and Learning, 8(2), 40-54.

Keltner, D., Oatley, K., & Jenkins, J. M. (2014). Understanding Emotions. Wiley.

Kowalski, R. M., Giumetti, G. W., & Schroeder, A. N. (2014). Bullying in the digital age: A critical review and meta-analysis of cyberbullying research among youth. Psychological Bulletin, 140(4), 1073-1137.

Kowert, R. (2020). The psychology of online gaming: Cyberbullying, empathy, and regulation. Journal of Youth Studies, 23(9), 1245-1260.

Kraft, M. A., & Gollust, S. E. (2021). Parents' perceptions of media use: A framework for understanding family media agreements. Journal of Family Issues, 42(2), 324-346.

Lange, J. (2020). Navigating difficult conversations with your child: A guide for parents. Parenting Today, 34(2), 56-60.

Livingstone, S., Haddon, L., Görzig, A., & Ólafsson, K. (2011). Risks and Safety on the Internet: The Perspective of European Children. EU Kids Online.

Livingstone, S., & Smith, P. K. (2014). Annual review of cyberbullying research: Findings and trends. Journal of Child Psychology and Psychiatry, 55(4), 376-385.

Livingstone, S., Stoilova, M., & Nandi, A. (2017). Children's online activities, risks, and safety: A European perspective. European Journal of Communication, 32(5), 487-502.

Luthar, S. S., Cicchetti, D., & Becker, B. (2000). The construct of resilience: A critical evaluation and guidelines for future work. Child Development, 71(3), 543-562.

Masten, A. S. (2001). Community resilience: Concepts and findings. In Handbook of Resilience in Children (pp. 1-26). Springer.

Mayer, J. D., & Salovey, P. (1997). What is emotional intelligence? In P. Salovey & D. J. Sluyter (Eds.), Emotional Development and Emotional Intelligence: Educational Implications (pp. 3-31). Basic Books.

Mihailidis, P., & Thevenin, B. (2013). Media literacy as a tool for democratic engagement. Journal of Media Literacy Education, 5(1), 1-11.

Miller, A. L. (2022). Navigating family dynamics in the digital age: Strategies for healthy media use. Family Relations, 71(1), 33-50.

Nolen-Hoeksema, S. (2001). Gender differences in depression. Current Directions in Psychological Science, 10(5), 173-176.

O'Connell, P., Pepler, D. J., & Craig, W. M. (2013). Bullying and peer victimization in children and youth: A developmental perspective. Canadian Psychology/Psychologie canadienne, 54(3), 178-186.

O'Reilly, M., & Dogra, N. (2020). Understanding cyberbullying: A parent's guide to online safety. Social Work in Education, 39(1), 29-38.

Peterson, C., & Seligman, M. E. P. (2004). Character Strengths and Virtues: A Handbook and Classification. American Psychological Association.

Pellegrini, A. D., & Long, J. D. (2002). A longitudinal study of bullying, dominance, and victimization during the transition from primary school through secondary school. British Journal of Developmental Psychology, 20(2), 259-280.

Polites, G. L., et al. (2021). The effects of positive social interactions on online engagement: A longitudinal study. Computers in Human Behavior, 122, 106859.

Pouwels, J. L., et al. (2018). The influence of social norms on adolescents' cyberbullying behavior: A systematic review and meta-analysis. Cyberpsychology, Behavior, and Social Networking, 21(8), 521-528

Ribble, M. (2015). Digital citizenship in schools. International Society for Technology in Education.

Ribble, M., & Bailey, G. (2007). Digital citizenship in schools: Nine elements all students should know. International Society for Technology in Education.

Rivers, I., & Noret, N. (2010). Bullying and cyberbullying: Experiences of undergraduate students. Journal of Aggression, Conflict and Peace Research, 2(4), 1-16.

Seçilmiş, A., & Çakır, M. (2017). The role of social status in the cyberbullying behavior of adolescents. Journal of Education and Practice, 8(14), 33-39.

Simmons, J. (2020). Building trust with children: Strategies for parents in the digital age. Journal of Family Studies, 26(4), 471-482.

Schmidt, C., et al. (2016). Self-esteem and bullying: A meta-analytic review. Aggression and Violent Behavior, 31, 49-62.

Smith, P. K., Mahdavi, J., & Carvalho, M. (2008). Cyberbullying: Its nature and impact in secondary school pupils. Journal of Child Psychology and Psychiatry, 49(4), 376-385.

Snyder, C. R. (2000). The Psychology of Hope: You Can Get There from Here. Free Press.

Tokunaga, R. S. (2010). Following you home from school: A critical review and synthesis of research on cyberbullying victimization. Computers in Human Behavior, 26(3), 277-287.

Wang, J., Nansel, T. R., & Iannotti, R. J. (2011). Cyber and traditional bullying: Differential association with depression. Journal of Adolescent Health, 48(2), 127-129.

Willard, N. (2007). Cyberbullying and cyberthreats: Responding to the challenge of online social cruelty, threats, and distress. Research Press.

Wong, C. H., & McKenzie, K. J. (2020). Family communication about internet safety: A developmental perspective. Journal of Family Communication, 20(3), 171-185.

Wright, M. F., & Wachs, S. (2019). Parental mediation and cyberbullying: A longitudinal study of the role of online safety, parenting styles, and empathy. Computers in Human Behavior, 91, 261-272.

www.ingramcontent.com/pod-product-compliance
Lightning Source LLC
Chambersburg PA
CBHW052257220526
45471CB00001B/377